WHAT'S COOKING
Italian

Penny Stephens

This edition published
in 1999 by
Parragon
Queen Street House
4 Queen Street
Bath BA1 1HE

ISBN: 0-75252-933-1 (Paperback)
ISBN: 0-75253-229-4 (Hardback)

Printed in Singapore

Produced by Haldane Mason, London

Acknowledgements
Art Director: Ron Samuels
Editorial Director: Sydney Francis
Editorial Consultant: Christopher Fagg
Managing Editor: Jo-Anne Cox
Editor: Lydia Darbyshire
Design: Digital Artworks Partnership Ltd
Photography: Iain Bagwell
Home Economist: Penny Stephens
Home Economist's Assistants: Nicky Deeley, Jean Stephens

Note
Cup measurements in this book are for American cups.
Tablespoons are assumed to be 15 ml. Unless otherwise stated,
milk is assumed to be full fat, eggs are medium
and pepper is freshly ground black pepper.

Contents

Introduction

There are two main culinary zones in Italy: the wine and olive zone, which lies around Umbria, Liguria, and the South; and the cattle country, where the olive tree will not flourish – Emilia-Romagna, Lombardy, and Veneto – but where milk and butter are widely produced. Tuscany, however, is the exception – it uses both butter and oil in its cooking because both cattle and olive trees thrive in the area.

ITALIAN FOOD REGION BY REGION

Piedmont

The food here is substantial, peasant-type fare, although the expensive fragrant white truffle is found in this region. Truffles can be finely flaked or grated and added to many of the more sophisticated dishes. There is an abundance of wild mushrooms throughout the region. Garlic features strongly in the recipes and polenta, gnocchi, and rice are eaten in larger quantities than pasta, the former being offered as a first course when soup is not served. A large variety of game is also widely available.

Lombardy

Milan is home to the wonderful risotto named after the city and also the Milanese soufflé flavoured strongly with lemon. Veal dishes, including *vitello tonnato* and *osso buco*, are specialties of the region and other excellent meat dishes, particularly pot roasts, feature widely. The lakes of the area produce a wealth of fresh fish. Rice and polenta are again popular but pasta also appears in many guises. The famous sweet yeasted cake *panettone* is a product of this region.

Trentino-Alto Adige

The foods are robust and basic here, where fish are plentiful. In the Trentino area particularly, pasta and simple meat dishes are popular, while in the Adige, soups and pot roasts are favoured, often with added dumplings and spiced sausages.

Veneto

Polenta is served with almost everything here. The land is intensively farmed, providing mostly cereals and wine. Pasta is less in evidence, with gnocchi and rice more favoured. Fish, particularly shellfish, is in abundance and especially good seafood salads are widely available. There are also excellent robust soups and risottos flavoured with the seafood and sausages of the area.

Liguria

All along the Italian Riviera can be found excellent trattorias which produce amazing fish dishes flavoured with the local olive oil. Pesto sauce flavoured with basil, cheese, and pine nuts comes from this area, along with other excellent sauces. Fresh herbs abound, widely used in many dishes, including the famous pizzas.

Emilia-Romagna

Tortellini and lasagne feature widely here, along with many other pasta dishes, as do *saltimbocca* and other veal dishes. Parma is famous for its ham, *prosciutto di Parma*, thought to be the best in the world. Balsamic vinegar is also produced here, from wine which is distilled until it is dark brown and extremely strongly flavoured.

Tuscany

Tuscany has everything: an excellent coastal area providing splendid fish, hills covered in vineyards, and fertile plains where every conceivable vegetable and fruit grows. There is plenty of game in the region, providing many interesting recipes; tripe cooked in a thick tomato sauce is popular along with many liver recipes; beans in many guises appear frequently, as well as pot roasts, steaks, and full-bodied soups, all of which are well flavoured. Florence has a wide variety of specialties, while Siena boasts the famous candied fruit cake called *Panforte di Siena*.

Umbria/Marches

Inland Umbria is famous for its pork, and the character of the cuisine is marked by the use of the local fresh ingredients, including lamb, game, and fish from the lakes. Spit-roasting and broiling is popular, and the excellent local olive oil is used both in cooking and to pour over dishes before serving. Black truffles, olives, fruit, and herbs are plentiful and feature in many recipes. First-class sausages and cured pork come from the Marches, particularly on the Umbrian border, and pasta features all over the region.

Lazio

Here, there are many pasta dishes with delicious sauces, gnocchi in various forms, and plenty of dishes featuring lamb and veal (*saltimbocca* being just one), and a variety of meats, all with plenty of herbs and seasonings giving really robust flavours and delicious sauces. Vegetables feature along with fantastic fruits; and beans appear both in soups and many other dishes.

Abruzzi and Molise

The cuisine here is deeply traditional, with local hams and cheeses from the mountain areas, interesting sausages with plenty of garlic and other seasonings, cured meats, and wonderful fish and seafood. Lamb features widely: tender, juicy, and well-flavoured with herbs.

Campania

Naples is the home of pasta dishes, served with a splendid tomato sauce (with many variations). Pizza is said to have been created in Naples. Fish abounds, with *fritto misto* and *fritto pesce* being great favourites. Fish stews are robust and varied and shellfish in particular is often served with pasta. Cutlets and steaks are excellent, served with strong sauces flavoured with garlic, tomatoes, and herbs: pizzaiola steak is one of the favourites. Mozzarella cheese is produced locally and used to create the crispy Mozzarella in Carozza, again served with a garlicky tomato sauce. Sweet dishes are popular too, often with flaky pastry and Ricotta cheese, and the seasonal fruit salads are laced with wine or liqueur.

Puglia (Apulia)

The ground in this region is stony but it produces good fruit, olive groves, vegetables, and herbs, and, of course, there is a large amount of seafood from the sea. Many of the excellent pasta dishes are exclusive to the region both in shape and ingredients. Mushrooms abound and are always added to the local pizzas. Oysters and mussels are plentiful, and so is octopus. Brindisi is famous for its shellfish – both the seafood salads and risottos are truly memorable. But it is not all fish or pasta: lamb is roasted and stewed to perfection and so is veal, always with plenty of herbs.

Basilicata

Here potent wines are produced to accompany a robust cuisine largely based on pasta, lamb, pork, game, and abundant dairy produce. The salamis and cured meats are excellent, as are the mountain hams. Lamb is flavoured with the herbs and grasses on which it feeds. Wonderful thick soups – true minestrone – are produced in the mountains, and eels and fish are plentiful in the lakes. Chilli peppers are grown in this region and appear in many of the recipes. The cheeses are excellent, good fruit is grown, and interesting local bread is baked in huge loaves.

Calabria

This is the toe of Italy, where orange and lemon groves flourish along with olive trees and a profusion of vegetables, especially aubergines (eggplants) which are cooked in a variety of ways. Chicken, rabbit, and guinea fowl are often on the menu. Pizzas feature largely, often with a fishy topping. Mushrooms grow well in the Calabrian climate and feature in many dishes from sauces and stews to salads. Pasta comes with a great variety of sauces including baby artichokes, eggs, meat, cheese, mixed vegetables, the large sweet (bell) peppers of the region, and of course garlic. The fish is excellent too and fresh tuna and swordfish are available, along with many other varieties. Many desserts and cakes are flavoured with aniseed, honey, and almonds and feature the plentiful figs of the region.

Sicily

This is the largest island in the Mediterranean and the cuisine is based mainly on fish and vegetables. Fish soups, stews, and salads appear in unlimited forms, including tuna, swordfish, mussels, and many more; citrus fruits are widely grown along with almonds and pistachio nuts, and the local wines, including the dark, sweet, dessert wine Marsala, are excellent. Meat is often given a long, slow cooking, or else is ground and shaped before cooking. Game is plentiful and is often cooked in sweet-sour sauces containing the local black olives. Pasta abounds again with more unusual sauces as well as the old favourites. All Sicilians have a love of desserts, cakes, and especially ice-cream. *Cassata* and other ice-creams from Sicily are famous all over the world.

Sardinia

The national dish of Sardinia is suckling pig or newborn lamb cooked on an open fire or spit, and rabbit, game, and a variety of meat dishes are also very popular. There is fresh fruit of almost every kind in abundance. Fish is also top quality, with excellent sea bass, lobsters, tuna, mullet, eels, and mussels in good supply. Myrtle (*mirto*), a local herb, is added to everything from chicken dishes to the local liqueur; and along with the cakes and breads of Sardinia, myrtle will long remain a fond memory of the island when you have returned home.

Starters & Snacks

Soups are an important part of Italian cuisine. They vary in consistency from light and delicate starters to hearty main meal soups. Although some may be puréed the ingredients never lose their delicious flavour.

Antipasto *means 'before the main course' and what is served may be simple and inexpensive or highly elaborate. It usually comes in three categories: meat, fish and vegetables. There are many varieties of cold meats, including ham, invariably sliced paper thin. All varieties of fish are enjoyed by the Italians, fresh sardines are particularly popular. Cook vegetables only until 'al dente' and still slightly crisp so that they retain more nutrients and the colours remain bright.*

Use plenty of colour – (bell) peppers, mangetout (snow peas) and baby corn cobs are all readily available. Use Italian staples, such as extra-virgin olive oil and balsamic vinegar for a salad dressing, and sprinkle over Italian cheeses, such as Parmesan and Pecorino.

This chapter also contains a range of delicious side dishes which will complement your main meal. Whatever you are looking for to tempt those tastebuds, you are sure to find it amongst these delicious delicacies.

Tuscan Bean Soup

A thick and creamy soup that is based on a traditional Tuscan recipe.
It is delicious served with fresh, warm bread and butter.

Serves 4

INGREDIENTS

225 g/8 oz dried butter beans soaked overnight or 2 x 420 g/14^1/$_2$ oz can butter beans

1 tbsp olive oil

2 garlic cloves, crushed

1 vegetable or chicken stock cube, crumbled

150 ml/5 fl oz/^{2}/$_3$ cup milk

2 tbsp chopped fresh oregano

salt and pepper

1 If you are using dried beans that have been soaked overnight, drain them thoroughly. Bring a large pan of water to the boil, add the beans and boil for 10 minutes. Cover the pan and simmer for a further 30 minutes or until tender. Drain the beans, reserving the cooking liquid. If you are using canned beans, drain them thoroughly and reserve the liquid.

2 Heat the oil in a large frying pan (skillet) and fry the garlic for 2–3 minutes or until just beginning to brown.

3 Add the beans and 400 ml/ 14 fl oz/1^2/$_3$ cup of the reserved liquid to the pan (skillet), stirring. You may need to add a little water if there is insufficient liquid. Stir in the crumbled stock cube. Bring the mixture to the boil and then remove the pan from the heat.

4 Place the bean mixture in a food processor and blend to form a smooth purée. Alternatively, mash the bean mixture to a smooth consistency. Season to taste with salt and pepper and stir in the milk.

5 Pour the soup back into the pan and gently heat to just below boiling point. Stir in the chopped oregano just before serving.

VARIATION

If you prefer, use 3 teaspoons of dried oregano instead of fresh, but add with the beans in step 3. This soup can also be made with cannelini or borlotti beans following the same method.

Brown Lentil Soup with Pasta

In Italy, this soup is called Minestrade Lentiche. *A* minestra *is a soup cooked with pasta; in this case farfalline, a small bow-shaped variety, is used. Served with lentils, this hearty soup is a meal in itself.*

Serves 4

INGREDIENTS

4 rashers streaky bacon, cut into
   small squares
1 onion, chopped
2 garlic cloves, crushed

2 sticks celery, chopped
50 g/1³/4 oz/¹/4 cup farfalline or
   spaghetti broken into small pieces
1 x 420 g/14¹/2 oz can brown lentils,
   drained

1.2 litres/2 pints/5 cups hot ham or
   vegetable stock
2 tbsp chopped, fresh mint

1 Place the bacon in a large frying pan (skillet) together with the onions, garlic and celery. Dry fry for 4–5 minutes, stirring, until the onion is tender and the bacon is just beginning to brown.

2 Add the farfalline or spaghetti pieces to the pan (skillet) and cook, stirring, for about 1 minute to coat the pasta in the oil.

3 Add the lentils and the stock and bring to the boil. Reduce the heat and leave to simmer for 12–15 minutes or until the pasta is tender.

4 Remove the pan (skillet) from the heat and stir in the chopped fresh mint.

5 Transfer the soup to warm soup bowls and serve immeditely.

COOK'S TIP

If you prefer to use dried lentils, add the stock before the pasta and cook for 1–1¹/4 hours until the lentils are tender. Add the pasta and cook for a further 12–15 minutes.

VARIATION

Any type of pasta can be used in this recipe, try fusilli, conchiglie or rigatoni, if you prefer.

Vegetable Soup with Cannelini Beans

*This wonderful combination of beans, vegetables and vermicelli is
made even richer by the addition of pesto and dried mushrooms.*

Serves 4

INGREDIENTS

1 small aubergine (eggplant)
2 large tomatoes
1 potato, peeled
1 carrot, peeled
1 leek
420 g/14^1/2 oz can cannelini beans

850 ml/1^1/2 pints/3^3/4 cups hot
  vegetable or chicken stock
2 tsp dried basil
10 g/^{1}/2 oz dried porcini mushrooms,
  soaked for 10 minutes in enough
  warm water to cover

50 g/1^3/4 oz/^{1}/4 cup vermicelli
3 tbsp pesto (see page 110 or use
  shop bought)
freshly grated Parmesan cheese, to
  serve (optional)

1 Slice the aubergine (eggplant) into rings about 10 mm/ ^{1}/2 inch thick, then cut each ring into 4.

2 Cut the tomatoes and potato into small dice. Cut the carrot into sticks, about 2.5 cm/ 1 inch long and cut the leek into rings.

3 Place the cannelini beans and their liquid in a large saucepan. Add the aubergine (eggplant), tomatoes, potatoes, carrot and leek, stirring to mix.

4 Add the stock to the pan and bring to the boil. Reduce the heat and leave to simmer for 15 minutes.

5 Add the basil, dried mushrooms, their soaking liquid and the vermicelli and simmer for 5 minutes or until all of the vegetables are tender.

6 Remove the pan from the heat and stir in the pesto.

7 Serve with freshly grated Parmesan cheese, if using.

COOK'S TIP

Porcini are a wild mushroom grown in southern Italy. When dried and rehydrated they have a very intense flavour, so although they are expensive to buy only a small amount are required to add flavour to soups or risottos.

Creamy Tomato Soup

This quick and easy creamy soup has a lovely fresh tomato flavour.

Serves 4

INGREDIENTS

50 g/1³/₄ oz/3 tbsp butter
700 g/1 lb 9oz ripe tomatoes,
   preferably plum, roughly chopped

850 ml/1¹/₂ pints/3³/₄ hot vegetable
   stock
150 ml/ 5 fl oz/²/₃ cup milk or single
   (light) cream

50 g/1³/₄ oz/¹/₄ cup ground almonds
1 tsp sugar
2 tbsp shredded basil leaves
salt and pepper

1 Melt the butter in a large saucepan. Add the tomatoes and cook for 5 minutes until the skins start to wrinkle. Season to taste with salt and pepper.

2 Add the stock to the pan, bring to the boil, cover and simmer for 10 minutes.

3 Meanwhile, under a preheated grill (broiler), lightly toast the ground almonds until they are golden-brown. This will take only 1-2 minutes, so watch them closely.

4 Remove the soup from the heat and place in a food processor and blend the mixture to form a smooth consistency. Alternatively, mash the soup with a potato masher.

5 Pass the soup through a sieve to remove any tomato skin or pips.

6 Place the soup in the pan and return to the heat. Stir in the milk or cream, ground almonds and sugar. Warm the soup through and add the shredded basil just before serving.

7 Transfer the creamy tomato soup to warm soup bowls and serve hot.

VARIATION

Very fine breadcrumbs can be used instead of the ground almonds, if you prefer. Toast them in the same way as the almonds and add with the milk or cream in step 6.

Tuscan Onion Soup

This soup is best made with white onions, which have a milder flavour than the more usual brown variety. If you cannot get hold of them, try using large Spanish onions instead.

Serves 4

INGREDIENTS

50 g/1³/₄ oz pancetta ham, diced
1 tbsp olive oil
4 large white onions, sliced thinly
   in rings
3 garlic cloves, chopped

850 ml/1³/₄ pints/3³/₄ cups hot
   chicken or ham stock
4 slices ciabatta or other Italian
   bread
50 g/1³/₄ oz/3 tbsp butter

75 g/2³/₄ oz Gruyère or Cheddar
salt and pepper

1 Dry fry the pancetta in a large saucepan for 3–4 minutes until it begins to brown. Remove the pancetta from the pan and set aside until required.

2 Add the oil to the pan and cook the onions and garlic over a high heat for 4 minutes. Reduce the heat, cover and cook for 15 minutes until lightly caramelized.

3 Add the stock to the saucepan and bring to the boil. Reduce the heat and leave the mixture to simmer, covered, for about 10 minutes.

4 Toast the slices of ciabatta on both sides, under a preheated grill (broiler), for 2–3 minutes or until golden. Spread the ciabatta with butter and top with the Gruyère or Cheddar cheese. Cut the bread into bite-size pieces.

5 Add the reserved pancetta to the soup and season to taste with salt and pepper. Pour into 4 soup bowls and top with the toasted bread.

COOK'S TIP

Pancetta is similar to bacon, but it is air- and salt-cured for about 6 months. Pancetta is available from most delicatessens and some large supermarkets. If you cannot obtain pancetta use unsmoked bacon instead.

Green Soup

*This fresh-tasting soup with green (dwarf) beans, cucumber and watercress
can be served warm or chilled on a hot summer day.*

Serves 4

INGREDIENTS

1 tbsp olive oil
1 onion, chopped
1 garlic clove, chopped
200 g/7 oz potato, peeled and cut
  into 2.5 cm/1 inch cubes

700 ml/1^{1}/$_{4}$ pint/scant 3 cups
  vegetable or chicken stock
1 small cucumber or ^{1}/$_{2}$ large
  cucumber, cut into chunks

80 g/3 oz bunch watercress
125 g/4^{1}/$_{2}$ oz green (dwarf) beans,
  trimmed and halved in length
salt and pepper

1 Heat the oil in a large pan
and fry the onion and garlic
for 3–4 minutes or until softened.
Add the cubed potato and fry for
a further 2–3 minutes.

2 Stir in the stock, bring to
the boil and leave to simmer
for 5 minutes.

3 Add the cucumber to the
pan and cook for a further
3 minutes or until the potatoes are
tender. Test by inserting the tip of
a knife into the potato cubes – it
should pass through easily.

4 Add the watercress and allow
to wilt. Then place the soup
in a food processor and blend until
smooth. Alternatively, before
adding the watercress, mash the
soup with a potato masher and
push through a sieve, then chop
the watercress finely and stir into
the soup.

5 Bring a small pan of water to
the boil and steam the beans
for 3–4 minutes or until tender.

6 Add the beans to the soup,
season and warm through.

VARIATION

*Try using 125 g/4^{1}/$_{2}$ oz mange tout
(snow peas) instead of the beans,
if you prefer.*

Artichoke Soup

This refreshing chilled soup, is ideal for al fresco dining.

Serves 4

INGREDIENTS

1 tbsp olive oil	2 x 400 g/14 oz can artichoke hearts, drained	150 ml/5 fl oz/^{2}/$_3$ cup single (light) cream
1 onion, chopped	600 ml/1 pint/2^1/$_2$ cupshot vegetable stock	2 tbsp fresh thyme, stalks removed
1 garlic clove, crushed		2 sun-dried tomatoes, cut into strips

1 Heat the oil in a large saucepan and fry the chopped onion and crushed garlic until just softened.

2 Using a sharp knife, roughly chop the artichoke hearts. Add the artichoke pieces to the onion and garlic mixture in the pan. Pour in the hot vegetable stock, stirring.

3 Bring the mixture to the boil, then reduce the heat and leave to simmer, covered, for about 3 minutes.

4 Place the mixture into a food processor and blend until smooth. Alternatively, push the mixture through a sieve to remove any lumps.

5 Return the soup to the saucepan. Stir the single (light) cream and fresh thyme into the soup.

6 Transfer the soup to a large bowl, cover, and leave to chill in the refrigerator for about 3–4 hours.

7 Transfer the chilled soup to individual soup bowls and garnish with strips of sun-dried tomato. Serve with lots of fresh, crusty bread.

VARIATION

Try adding 2 tablespoons of dry vermouth, such as Martini, to the soup in step 5 if you wish.

Orange, Thyme & Pumpkin Soup

This thick, creamy soup has a wonderful, warming
golden colour. It is flavoured with orange and thyme.

Serves 4

INGREDIENTS

2 tbsp olive oil
2 medium onions, chopped
2 cloves garlic, chopped
900 g/2 lb pumpkin, peeled and cut
  into 2.5 cm/1 inch chunks

1.5 litres /2 ^{3}/$_4$ pints/6^1/$_4$ cups boiling
  vegetable or chicken stock
finely grated rind and juice of
  1 orange

3 tbsp fresh thyme, stalks removed
150 ml/5 fl oz/^{2}/$_3$ cup milk
salt and pepper
crusty bread, to serve

1 Heat the olive oil in a large saucepan. Add the onions to the pan and cook for 3–4 minutes or until softened. Add the garlic and pumpkin and cook for a further 2 minutes, stirring well.

2 Add the boiling vegetable or chicken stock, orange rind and juice and 2 tablespoons of the thyme to the pan. Leave to simmer, covered, for 20 minutes or until the pumpkin is tender.

3 Place the mixture in a food processor and blend until smooth. Alternatively, mash the mixture with a potato masher until smooth. Season to taste with salt and pepper.

4 Return the soup to the saucepan and add the milk. Reheat the soup for 3–4 minutes or until it is piping hot but not boiling. Sprinkle with the remaining fresh thyme just before serving.

5 Divide the soup among 4 warm soup bowls and serve with lots of fresh crusty bread.

COOK'S TIP

Pumpkins are usually large vegetables. To make things a little easier, ask the greengrocer to cut a chunk off for you. Alternatively, make double the quantity and freeze the soup for up to 3 months.

Minestrone

Minestrone translates as 'big soup' in Italian. It is made all over Italy, but this version comes from Livorno, a port on the western coast.

Serves 4

INGREDIENTS

1 tbsp olive oil
100 g/3¹/₂ oz pancetta ham, diced
2 medium onions, chopped
2 cloves garlic, crushed
1 potato, peeled and cut into
    10 mm/¹/₂ inch cubes
1 carrot, scraped and cut into chunks
1 leek, sliced into rings

¹/₄ green cabbage, shredded
1 stick celery, chopped
1 x 450 g/1 lb can chopped tomatoes
1 x 210 g/7 oz can flageolet `(small
    navy) beans, drained and rinsed
600 ml/1 pint/2¹/₂ cups hot ham or
    chicken stock diluted with 600 ml/
    1 pint/2¹/₂ cups boiling water

bouquet garni (2 bay leaves, 2 sprigs
    rosemary and 2 sprigs thyme, tied
    together)
salt and pepper
freshly grated Parmesan cheese,
    to serve

1 Heat the oil in a large saucepan. Add the diced pancetta, chopped onions and garlic and fry for about 5 minutes or until the onions are soft and golden.

2 Add the prepared potato, carrot, leek, cabbage and celery to the saucepan. Cook for a further 2 minutes, stirring frequently, to coat all of the vegetables in the oil.

3 Add the tomatoes, flageolet (small navy) beans, hot ham or chicken stock and bouquet garni to the pan, stirring to mix. Leave the soup to simmer, covered, for 15–20 minutes or until all of the vegetables are just tender.

4 Remove the bouquet garni, season with salt and pepper to taste and serve with plenty of freshly grated Parmesan.

VARIATION

Any combination of vegetables will work equally well in this soup. For a special minestrone, try adding 100 g/3¹/₂ oz Parma ham (prosciutto), shredded, in step 1.

Calabrian Mushroom Soup

The Calabrian Mountains in southern Italy provide large amounts of wild mushrooms.
They are rich in flavour and colour and make a wonderful soup.

Serves 4

INGREDIENTS

2 tbsp olive oil
1 onion, chopped
450g/1 lb mixed mushrooms, such as
   ceps, oyster and button

300 ml/$\frac{1}{2}$ pint/1$\frac{1}{4}$ cup milk
850 ml1$\frac{1}{2}$ pints/3$\frac{3}{4}$ cups hot
   vegetable stock
8 slices of rustic bread or French stick
50 g/1$\frac{3}{4}$ oz/3 tbsp butter, melted

2 garlic cloves, crushed
75 g/2$\frac{3}{4}$ oz Gruyère cheese, finely
   grated
salt and pepper

1 Heat the oil in a large frying pan (skillet) and cook the onion for 3–4 minutes or until soft and golden.

2 Wipe each mushroom with a damp cloth and cut any large mushrooms into smaller, bite-size pieces.

3 Add the mushrooms to the pan, stirring quickly to coat them in the oil.

4 Add the milk to the pan, bring to the boil, cover and leave to simmer for about

5 minutes. Gradually stir in the hot vegetable stock.

5 Under a preheated grill (broiler), toast the bread on both sides until golden.

6 Mix together the garlic and butter and spoon generously over the toast.

7 Place the toast in the bottom of a large tureen or divide it among 4 individual serving bowls and pour over the hot soup. Top with the grated Gruyère cheese and serve at once.

COOK'S TIP

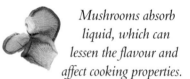

Mushrooms absorb liquid, which can lessen the flavour and affect cooking properties. Wipe them with a damp cloth rather than rinsing them in water.

VARIATION

Supermarkets stock a wide variety of wild mushrooms. If you prefer, use a combination of cultivated and wild mushrooms.

Tomatoes Stuffed with Tuna Mayonnaise

*Deliciously sweet roasted tomatoes are filled with
home-made lemon mayonnaise and tuna.*

Serves 4

INGREDIENTS

4 plum tomatoes
2 tbsp sun-dried tomato paste
2 egg yolks
2 tsp lemon juice
finely grated rind of 1 lemon

4 tbsp olive oil
1 x 115g/4 oz can tuna, drained
2 tbsp capers, rinsed
salt and pepper

TO GARNISH:
2 sun-dried tomatoes, cut into strips
fresh basil leaves

1 Halve the tomatoes and scoop out the seeds. Divide the sun-dried tomato paste among the tomato halves and spread around the inside of the skin.

2 Place on a baking tray (cookie sheet) and roast in a preheated oven at 200°C/400°F/ Gas Mark 6 for 12–15 minutes. Leave to cool slightly.

3 Meanwhile, make the mayonnaise. In a food processor, blend the egg yolks and lemon juice with the lemon rind until smooth. Once mixed and with the motor still running slowly, add the olive oil. Stop the processor as soon as the mayonnaise has thickened. Alternatively, use a hand whisk, beating the mixture continuously until it thickens.

4 Add the tuna and capers to the mayonnaise and season.

5 Spoon the tuna mayonnaise mixture into the tomato shells and garnish with sun-dried tomato strips and basil leaves. Return to the oven for a few minutes or serve chilled.

COOK'S TIP

For a picnic, do not roast the tomatoes, just scoop out the seeds, drain, cut-side down on absorbent kitchen paper for 1 hour, and fill with the mayonnaise mixture. They are firmer to handle and easier to eat with the fingers this way. If you prefer, shop-bought mayonnaise may be used instead – just stir in the lemon rind.

Deep-fried Risotto Balls

The Italian name for this dish translates as 'telephone wires' which refers to the strings of melted Mozzarella cheese, the surprise contained within the risotto balls.

Serves 4

INGREDIENTS

2 tbsp olive oil
1 medium onion, finely chopped
1 garlic clove, chopped
$^1/_2$ red (bell) pepper, diced

150 g/5 oz/$^3/_4$ cup arborio (risotto) rice, washed
1 tsp dried oregano
400 ml/14 fl oz/1$^2/_3$ cup hot vegetable or chicken stock

100 ml/3$^1/_2$ fl oz/$^1/_2$ scant cup dry white wine
75 g/2$^3/_4$ oz Mozzarella cheese
oil, for deep-frying
fresh basil sprig, to garnish

1 Heat the oil in a frying pan (skillet) and cook the onion and garlic for 3–4 minutes or until just softened.

2 Add the (bell) pepper, rice and oregano to the pan. Cook for 2–3 minutes, stirring to coat the rice in the oil.

3 Mix the stock together with the wine and add to the pan a ladleful at a time, waiting for the liquid to be absorbed by the rice before you add the next ladleful of liquid.

4 Once all of the liquid has been absorbed and the rice is tender (it should take about 15 minutes in total), remove the pan from the heat and leave until the mixture is cool enough to handle.

5 Cut the cheese into 12 pieces. Taking about a tablespoon of risotto, shape the mixture around the cheese pieces to make 12 balls.

6 Heat the oil until a piece of bread browns in 30 seconds. Cook the risotto balls in batches of 4 for 2 minutes until golden.

7 Remove the risotto balls with a perforated spoon and drain thoroughly on absorbent kitchen paper. Garnish with a sprig of basil and serve hot.

VARIATION

Although Mozzarella is the traditional cheese for this recipe and creates the stringy 'telephone wire' effect, other cheeses, such as Cheddar may be used if you prefer.

Black Olive Pâté

The flavour of olives is accentuated by the anchovies and the pâté is wonderful served as an appetizer on thin pieces of toast with a very dry white wine.

Serves 4

INGREDIENTS

175 g/6 oz black olives, pitted and chopped
finely grated rind and juice of 1 lemon

50 g/1½ oz unsalted butter
4 canned anchovy fillets, drained and rinsed

2 tbsp extra virgin olive oil
15 g/½ oz ground almonds

1 If you are making the pâté by hand, chop the olives very finely and then mash them along with the lemon rind, juice and butter, using a fork or potato masher. Alternatively, place the roughly chopped olives, lemon rind, juice and butter in a food processor and blend until all of the ingredients are finely chopped.

2 Using a sharp knife, chop the drained anchovies and add them to the olive and lemon mixture. Mash the pâté by hand or blend it in a food processor for about 20 seconds.

3 Gradually whisk in the olive oil and stir in the ground almonds. Place the black olive pâté in a serving bowl.

4 Leave the pâté to chill in the refrigerator for about 30 minutes. Serve accompanied by thin pieces of toast.

COOK'S TIP

Extra-virgin olive oil is the finest grade of olive oil. It is made from the first, cold pressing of hand gathered olives.

COOK'S TIP

The pâté will keep for up to 5 days in a serving bowl in the refrigerator if you pour a thin layer of extra-virgin olive oil over the top of the pâté to seal it. Then use the oil to brush on the toast before spreading the pâté.

Fresh Figs with Parma Ham (Prosciutto)

This colourful fresh salad is delicious at any time of the year.

Serves 4

INGREDIENTS

40 g/1¹/₂ oz rocket (arugula)
4 fresh figs
4 slices Parma ham (prosciutto)

4 tbsp olive oil
1 tbsp fresh orange juice

1 tbsp clear honey
1 small red chilli

1 Tear the rocket (arugula) into more manageable pieces and arrange on 4 serving plates.

2 Using a sharp knife, cut each of the figs into quarters and place them on top of the rocket (arugula) leaves.

3 Using a sharp knife, cut the Parma ham (prosciutto) into strips and scatter over the rocket (arugula) and figs.

4 Place the oil, orange juice and honey in a screw-top jar. Shake the jar until the mixture emulsifies and forms a thick dressing. Transfer to a bowl.

5 Using a sharp knife, dice the chilli, remembering not to touch your face before you have washed your hands (see Cook's Tip, right). Add the chopped chilli to the dressing and mix well.

6 Drizzle the dressing over the Parma ham (prosciutto), rocket (arugula) and figs, tossing to mix well. Serve at once.

COOK'S TIP

Parma, in the Emilia-Romagna region of Italy, is famous for its ham, prosciutto di Parma, thought to be the best in the world.

COOK'S TIP

Chillies can burn the skin for several hours after chopping, so it is advisable to wear gloves when you are handling the very hot varieties.

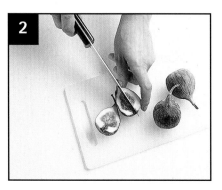

Roasted (Bell) Peppers

These (bell) peppers can be used as an antipasto, as a side dish or as a relish to accompany meat and fish.

Serves 4

INGREDIENTS

2 each, red, yellow and orange (bell) peppers
4 tomatoes, halved

1 tbsp olive oil
3 garlic cloves, chopped
1 onion, sliced in rings

2 tbsp fresh thyme
salt and pepper

1 Halve and deseed the (bell) peppers. Place them, cut-side down, on a baking tray (cookie sheet) and cook under a preheated grill (broiler) for 10 minutes.

2 Add the tomatoes to the baking tray (cookie sheet) and grill (broil) for 5 minutes, until the skins of the (bell) peppers and tomatoes are charred.

3 Put the (bell) peppers into a polythene bag for 10 minutes to sweat, which will make the skin easier to peel. Remove the tomato skins and roughly chop the flesh.

4 Peel the skins from the (bell) peppers and slice the flesh into strips.

5 Heat the oil in a large frying pan (skillet) and fry the garlic and onion for 3–4 minutes or until softened.

6 Add the (bell) peppers and tomatoes to the frying pan (skillet) and cook for 5 minutes. Stir in the fresh thyme and season to taste with salt and pepper.

7 Transfer to serving bowls and serve warm or chilled.

COOK'S TIP

You can preserve the (bell) peppers in the refrigerator by placing them in a sterilized jar and pouring olive oil over the top to seal. Alternatively, heat 300 ml/^{1}/$_2$ pint/^{1}/$_4$ cup white wine vinegar with a bay leaf and 4 juniper berries and bring to the boiling point. Pour over the (bell) peppers and set aside until completely cold. Pack into sterilized jars – they will keep for up to 1 month.

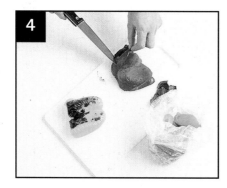

Baked Aubergines (Eggplant) & Tomatoes

This dish is a bit like an aubergine (eggplant) lasagne with layers of aubergine (eggplant), tomato sauce and Mozzarella combining with Parmesan cheese to create a wonderfully tasty starter.

Serves 4

INGREDIENTS

3–4 tbsp olive oil
2 garlic cloves, crushed
2 large aubergines (eggplants)

100 g/3 1/2 oz Mozzarella cheese,
  sliced thinly
200 g/7 oz passata (tomato purée)

50 g/1 3/4 oz Parmesan cheese, grated

1 Heat 2 tablespoons of the olive oil in a large frying pan (skillet). Add the garlic to the frying pan (skillet) and sauté for 30 seconds.

2 Slice the aubergines (eggplants) lengthwise. Add the slices to the pan and cook in the oil for 3–4 minutes on each side or until tender. (You will probably have to cook them in batches, so add the remaining oil as necessary.)

3 Remove the aubergines (eggplants) with a perforated spoon and drain on absorbent kitchen paper.

4 Place a layer of aubergine (eggplant) slices in a shallow ovenproof dish. Cover the aubergines (eggplants) with a layer of Mozzarella and then pour over a third of the passata (tomato purée). Continue layering in the same order, finishing with a layer of passata (tomato purée) on top.

5 Generously sprinkle the grated Parmesan cheese over the top and bake in a preheated oven at 200°C/400°F/Gas Mark 6 for 25–30 minutes.

6 Transfer to serving plates and serve warm or chilled.

COOK'S TIP

Passata (tomato purée) is a simple tomato sauce, which can be bought from most supermarkets. Alternatively, you can purée and sieve a can of tomatoes and season with salt and pepper.

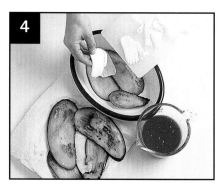

Courgette (Zucchini) & Thyme Fritters

*These tasty little fritters are great with roasted (bell) peppers
(see page 36) as a relish for a drinks party.*

Makes: 16 medium-sized fritters or about 30 small-sized fritters

INGREDIENTS

100 g/3¹/₂ oz self-raising flour
2 eggs, beaten
50 ml/2 fl oz milk

300 g/10¹/₂ oz courgettes (zucchini)
2 tbsp fresh thyme

1 tbsp oil
salt and pepper

---

1 Sift the self-raising flour into a large bowl and make a well in the centre. Add the egg to the well, and using a wooden spoon, gradually draw in the flour.

2 Slowly add the milk to the mixture, stirring constantly to form a thick batter.

3 Meanwhile, wash the courgettes (zucchini). Grate the courgettes (zucchini) over a sheet of kitchen paper placed in a bowl to absorb some of the juices.

4 Add the courgettes (zucchini), thyme, salt and pepper to taste to the batter and mix thoroughly.

5 Heat the oil in a large, heavy-based frying pan (skillet). Taking a tablespoon of the batter for a medium-sized fritter or half a tablespoon of batter for a smaller-sized fritter, spoon the mixture into the hot oil and cook, in batches, for 3–4 minutes on each side.

6 Remove the fritters with a perforated spoon and drain thoroughly on absorbent kitchen paper. Keep each batch of fritters warm in the oven while making the rest. Serve hot.

VARIATION

Try adding ¹/₂ teaspoon of dried, crushed chillies in step 4 for spicier tasting fritters.

Cured Meats with Olives & Tomatoes

This is a typical antipasto dish with the cold cured meats, stuffed olives and fresh tomatoes, basil and balsamic vinegar.

Serves 4

INGREDIENTS

4 plum tomatoes
1 tbsp balsamic vinegar
6 canned anchovy fillets, drained and rinsed

2 tbsp capers, drained and rinsed
125 g/4¹/2 oz green olives, pitted
175 g/6 oz mixed, cured meats, sliced
8 fresh basil leaves

1 tbsp extra virgin olive oil
salt and pepper
crusty bread, to serve

1 Using a sharp knife, cut the tomatoes into evenly-sized slices. Sprinkle the tomato slices with the balsamic vinegar and a little salt and pepper to taste and set aside.

2 Chop the anchovy fillets into pieces measuring about the same length as the olives.

3 Push a piece of anchovy and a caper into each olive.

4 Arrange the sliced meat on 4 individual serving plates together with the tomatoes, filled olives and basil leaves.

5 Lightly drizzle the olive oil over the sliced meat, tomatoes and olives.

6 Serve the cured meats, olives and tomatoes with lots of fresh crusty bread.

COOK'S TIP

The cured meats for this recipe are up to your individual taste. They can include a selection of Parma ham (prosciutto), pancetta, bresaola (dried salt beef) and salame di Milano (pork and beef sausage.

COOK'S TIP

Fill a screw-top jar with the stuffed olives, cover with olive oil and use when required – they will keep for 1 month in the refrigerator.

Spinach & Ricotta Patties

'Nudo' or naked is the word used to describe this mixture, which can also be made into thin pancakes or used as a filling for tortelloni.

Serves 4

INGREDIENTS

450 g/1 lb fresh spinach
250 g/9 oz ricotta cheese
1 egg, beaten
2 tsp fennel seeds, lightly crushed

50 g/1 3/4 oz pecorino or Parmesan
  cheese, finely grated
25 g/1 oz plain (all-purpose) flour,
  mixed with 1 tsp dried thyme
75 g/2 3/4 oz/5 tbsp butter

2 garlic cloves, crushed
salt and pepper

1 Wash the spinach and trim off any long stalks. Place in a pan, cover and cook for 4–5 minutes until wilted. This will probably have to be done in batches as the volume of spinach is quite large. Place in a colander and leave to drain and cool.

2 Mash the ricotta and beat in the egg and the fennel seeds. Season with plenty of salt and pepper, then stir in the pecorino or Parmesan cheese.

3 Squeeze as much excess water as possible from the spinach and finely chop the leaves. Stir into the cheese mixture.

4 Taking about 1 tablespoon of the spinach and cheese mixture, shape it into a ball and flatten it slightly to form a patty. Gently roll in the seasoned flour. Continue this process until all of the mixture has been used up.

5 Half fill a large frying pan (skillet) with water and bring to the boil. Carefully add the patties and cook for 3–4 minutes or until they rise to the surface. Remove with a perforated spoon.

6 Melt the butter in a pan. Add the garlic and cook for 2–3 minutes. Pour the garlic butter over the patties, season with freshly ground black pepper and serve at once.

COOK'S TIP

Once it is washed, spinach holds enough water on the leaves to cook without adding any extra liquid. If you use frozen spinach instead of fresh, simply defrost it and squeeze out the excess water.

Sweet & Sour Baby Onions

This is a typical Sicilian dish, combining honey and vinegar to give a delicate sweet and sour flavour. Serve hot as an accompaniment or cold with cured meats.

Serves 4

INGREDIENTS

350 g/12 oz baby or pickling onions
2 tbsp olive oil
2 fresh bay leaves, torn into strips

thinly pared rind of 1 lemon
1 tbsp soft brown sugar
1 tbsp clear honey

4 tbsp red wine vinegar

1 Soak the onions in a bowl of boiling water – this will make them easier to peel. Using a sharp knife, peel and halve the onions.

2 Heat the oil in a large frying pan (skillet). Add the bay leaves and onions to the pan and cook for 5–6 minutes over a medium-high heat or until browned all over.

3 Cut the lemon rind into thin matchsticks. Add to the frying pan (skillet) with the sugar and honey. Cook for 2-3 minutes, stirring occasionally, until the onions are lightly caramelized.

4 Add the red wine vinegar to the frying pan (skillet), being careful because it will spit. Cook for about 5 minutes, stirring, or until the onions are tender and the liquid has all but disappeared.

5 Transfer the onions to a serving dish and serve at once.

COOK'S TIP

Adjust the piquancy of this dish to your liking by adding more sugar for a sweeter, more caramelized taste or extra red wine vinegar for a sharper, tarter flavour.

COOK'S TIP

To make the onions easier to peel, place them in a large saucepan, pour over boiling water and leave for 10 minutes. Drain the onions thoroughly, and when they are cold enough to handle, peel them.

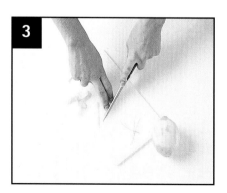

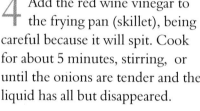

Stewed Artichokes

*This is a traditional Roman dish. The artichokes
are stewed in olive oil with fresh herbs.*

Serves 4

INGREDIENTS

4 small globe artichokes
4 garlic cloves, peeled

2 bay leaves
finely grated rind and juice of
1 lemon

olive oil
2 tbsp fresh marjoram
lemon wedges, to serve

1 Using a sharp knife, carefully peel away the tough outer leaves surrounding the artichokes. Trim the stems to about 2.5 cm/ 1 inch.

2 Using a knife, cut each artichoke in half and scoop out the choke (heart).

3 Place the artichokes in a large heavy based pan. Pour over enough olive oil to half cover the artichokes in the pan.

4 Add the garlic cloves, bay leaves and half of the grated lemon rind.

5 Start to heat the artichokes gently, cover the pan and continue to cook over a low heat for about 40 minutes. The artichokes should be stewed in the oil, not fried.

6 Once the artichokes are tender, remove them with a perforated spoon and drain thoroughly. Remove the bay leaves.

7 Transfer the artichokes to warm serving plates. Serve the artichokes sprinkled with the remaining grated lemon rind, fresh marjoram and a little lemon juice.

COOK'S TIP

To prevent the artichokes from oxidizing and turning brown before cooking, brush them with a little lemon juice. In addition, use the oil used for cooking the artichokes for salad dressings – it will impart a lovely lemon and herb flavour.

Chickpeas with Parma Ham (Prosciutto)

Prosciutto is a cured ham, which is air- and salt-dried for up to 1 year. There are many different varieties available, and the one used here is crudo, *which is slightly coarser than other types.*

Serves 4

INGREDIENTS

1 tbsp olive oil
1 medium onion, thinly sliced
1 garlic clove, chopped

1 small red (bell) pepper, deseeded
and cut into thin strips
200 g/7 oz Parma ham (prosciutto),
cut into chunks

1 x 400g/14 oz can chick peas,
drained and rinsed
1 tbsp chopped parsley, to garnish
crusty bread, to serve

1 Heat the oil in a large frying pan (skillet). Add the sliced onion, chopped garlic and sliced (bell) pepper and cook for 3–4 minutes or until the vegetables have softened.

2 Add the Parma ham (prosciutto) to the frying pan (skillet) and fry for 5 minutes or until the ham (prosciutto) is just beginning to brown.

3 Add the chickpeas to the frying pan (skillet) and cook, stirring, for 2–3 minutes until warmed through.

4 Sprinkle with chopped parsley and transfer to warm serving plates. Serve with lots of fresh crusty bread.

COOK'S TIP

Whenever possible, use fresh herbs when cooking. They are becoming more readily available, especially since the introduction of 'growing' herbs, small pots of herbs which you can buy from the supermarket or greengrocer and grow at home. This ensures the herbs are fresh and also provides a continuous supply.

VARIATION

Try adding a small finely diced chilli in step 1 for a spicier taste, if you prefer.

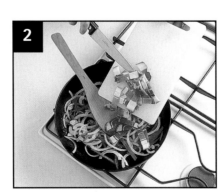

Deep-fried Seafood

*Deep-fried seafood is popular all around the Mediterranean, where fish of all kinds is
fresh and abundant. Serve with garlic mayonnaise and lemon wedges.*

Serves 4

INGREDIENTS

200 g/7 oz prepared squid
200 g/7 oz blue (raw) tiger prawns
(shrimp), peeled
150 g/5^1/$_2$ oz whitebait

oil, for deep-frying
50 g/1^1/$_2$ oz plain (all-purpose) flour
1 tsp dried basil
salt and pepper

TO SERVE:
garlic mayonnaise (see Cook's Tip)
lemon wedges

1 Carefully rinse the squid, prawns (shrimp) and whitebait under cold running water, completely removing any dirt or grit.

2 Using a sharp knife, slice the squid into rings, leaving the tentacles whole.

3 Heat the oil in a large saucepan to 180°–190°C/ 350°–375°F or until a cube of bread browns in 30 seconds.

4 Place the flour in a bowl and season with the salt, pepper and basil.

5 Roll the squid, prawns (shrimp) and whitebait in the seasoned flour until coated all over. Carefully shake off any excess flour.

6 Cook the seafood in the heated oil in batches for 2–3 minutes or until crispy and golden all over. Remove all of the seafood with a perforated spoon and leave to drain thoroughly on kitchen paper.

7 Transfer the deep-fried seafood to serving plates and serve with garlic mayonnaise (see Cook's Tip) and lemon wedges.

COOK'S TIP

To make garlic mayonnaise for serving with the deep-fried seafood, crush 2 garlic cloves, stir into 8 tablespoons of mayonnaise and season with salt and pepper and a little chopped parsley.

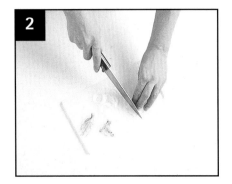

Tuscan Bean Salad with Tuna

The combination of beans and tuna is a favourite with the people of Tuscany. The hint of honey and lemon in the dressing makes this salad refreshing as well as hearty.

Serves 4

INGREDIENTS

1 small white onion or 2 spring
   onions (scallions), finely chopped
2 x 400g/14 oz cans butter beans,
   drained

2 medium tomatoes
1 x 185 g/6$^{1}/_{2}$ oz can tuna, drained
2 tbsp flat leaf parsley, chopped
2 tbsp olive oil

1 tbsp lemon juice
2 tsp clear honey
1 garlic clove, crushed

1 Place the chopped onions or spring onions (scallions) and butter beans in a bowl and mix well to combine.

2 Using a sharp knife, cut the tomatoes into wedges. Add the tomatoes to the onion and bean mixture.

3 Flake the tuna with a fork and add it to the onion and bean mixture together with the parsley.

4 In a screw-top jar, mix together the olive oil, lemon juice, honey and garlic. Shake the jar until the dressing emulsifies and thickens.

5 Pour the dressing over the bean salad. Toss the ingredients together using 2 spoons and serve.

COOK'S TIP

This salad will keep for several days in a covered container in the refrigerator. Make up the dressing just before serving and toss the ingredients together to mix well.

VARIATION

Substitute fresh salmon for the tuna if you wish to create a luxurious version of this recipe for a special occasion.

Italian Potato Salad

*Potato salad is always a favourite, but it is even more delicious
with the addition of sun-dried tomatoes and fresh parsley.*

Serves 4

INGREDIENTS

450g/1 lb baby potatoes, unpeeled, or
larger potatoes, halved
4 tbsp natural yogurt

4 tbsp mayonnaise
8 sun-dried tomatoes

2 tbsp flat leaf parsley, chopped
salt and pepper

1 Rinse and clean the potatoes and place them in a large pan of water. Bring to the boil and cook for 8–12 minutes or until just tender. (The cooking time will vary according to the size of your potatoes.)

2 Using a sharp knife, cut the sun-dried tomatoes into thin slices.

3 To make the dressing, mix together the yogurt and mayonnaise in a bowl and season to taste with a little salt and pepper. Stir in the sun-dried tomato slices and the chopped flat leaf parsley.

4 Remove the potatoes with a perforated spoon, drain them thoroughly and then set them aside to cool. If you are using larger potatoes, cut them into 5 cm/2 inch chunks.

5 Pour the dressing over the potatoes and toss to mix.

6 Leave the potato salad to chill in the refrigerator for about 20 minutes, then serve as a starter or as an accompaniment.

COOK'S TIP

It is easier to cut the larger potatoes once they are cooked.
Although smaller pieces of potato will cook more quickly, they tend to disintegrate and become mushy.

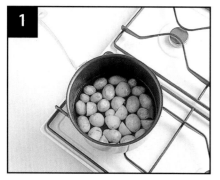

Green Salad

This is a green salad with a difference – herb-flavoured croûtons are topped with peppery rocket (arugula), red chard, green olives and pistachios to make an elegant combination.

Serves 4

INGREDIENTS

25 g/1 oz pistachio nuts
5 tbsp extra virgin olive oil
1 tbsp rosemary, chopped
2 garlic cloves, chopped
4 slices rustic bread

1 tbsp red wine vinegar
1 tsp wholegrain mustard
1 tsp sugar
25 g/1 oz rocket (arugula)
25 g/1 oz red chard

50 g/1³/₄ oz green olives, pitted
2 tbsp fresh basil, shredded

1 Shell the pistachios and roughly chop them, using a sharp knife.

2 Place 2 tablespoons of the extra virgin olive oil in a frying pan (skillet). Add the rosemary and garlic and cook for 2 minutes.

3 Add the slices of bread to the pan and fry for 2–3 minutes on both sides until golden. Remove the bread from the pan and leave to drain on absorbent kitchen paper.

4 To make the dressing, mix together the remaining olive oil with the red wine vinegar, mustard and sugar.

5 Place a slice of bread on to a serving plate and top with the rocket (arugula) and red chard. Sprinkle with the olives.

6 Drizzle the dressing over the top of the salad leaves. Sprinkle with the chopped pistachios and shredded basil leaves and serve the salad immediately.

COOK'S TIP

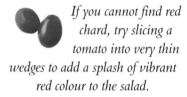

If you cannot find red chard, try slicing a tomato into very thin wedges to add a splash of vibrant red colour to the salad.

VARIATION

Watercress may be used instead of the rocket (arugula), if preferred.

Minted Fennel Salad

*This is a very refreshing salad. The subtle liquorice flavour of
fennel combines well with the cucumber and mint.*

Serves 4

INGREDIENTS

1 bulb fennel	1 small or ½ a large cucumber	1 tbsp virgin olive oil
2 small oranges	1 tbsp chopped mint	2 eggs, hard boiled (cooked)

1 Using a sharp knife, trim the outer leaves from the fennel. Slice the fennel bulb thinly into a bowl of water and sprinkle with lemon juice (see Cook's Tip).

2 Grate the rind of the oranges over a bowl. Using a sharp knife, pare away the orange peel, then segment the orange by carefully slicing between each line of pith. Do this over the bowl in order to retain the juice.

3 Using a sharp knife, cut the cucumber into 12 mm/ ½ inch rounds and then cut each round into quarters. Add the cucumber to the fennel and orange mixture together with the mint.

4 Pour the olive oil over the fennel and cucumber salad and toss well.

5 Peel and quarter the eggs and use these to decorate the top of the salad. Serve at once.

COOK'S TIP

Virgin olive oil, which has a fine aroma and flavour, is made by the cold pressing of olives. However, it may have a slightly higher acidity level than extra virgin oil.

COOK'S TIP

Fennel will discolour if it is left for any length of time without a dressing. To prevent any discoloration, place it in a bowl of water and sprinkle with lemon juice.

Capri Salad

This tomato, olive and Mozzarella salad, dressed with balsamic vinegar and olive oil, makes a delicious starter on its own. Increase the quantity by half to make for a full salad for four people.

Serves 4

INGREDIENTS

2 beef tomatoes
125 g/4^{1}/$_{2}$ oz Mozzarella cheese
12 black olives

8 basil leaves
1 tbsp balsamic vinegar
1 tbsp olive oil

salt and pepper
basil leaves, to garnish

1 Using a sharp knife, cut the tomatoes into thin slices.

2 Using a sharp knife, cut the Mozzarella into slices.

3 Pit the olives and slice them into rings.

4 Layer the tomato, Mozzarella cheese and olives in a stack, finishing with a layer of cheese on top.

5 Place each stack under a preheated hot grill (broiler) for 2–3 minutes or just long enough to melt the Mozzarella.

6 Drizzle over the vinegar and olive oil, and season to taste with salt and pepper.

7 Transfer to serving plates and garnish with basil leaves. Serve immediately.

COOK'S TIP

Buffalo mozzarella cheese, although it is usually more expensive because of the comparative rarity of buffalo, does have a better flavour than the cow's milk variety. It is popular in salads, but also provides a tangy layer in baked dishes.

COOK'S TIP

Balsamic vinegar, which has grown in popularity over the past decade, is produced in the Emilia-Romagna region of Italy. It is made from wine which is distilled until it is dark brown and extremely strongly flavoured.

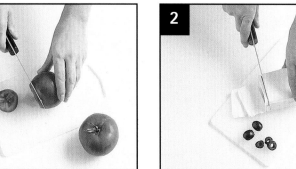

Mushroom Salad

*Raw mushrooms are a great favourite in Italian dishes –
they have a fresh, almost creamy flavour.*

Serves 4

INGREDIENTS

150 g/5^1/$_2$ oz firm white mushrooms
4 tbsp virgin olive oil

1 tbsp lemon juice
5 anchovy fillets, drained and
   chopped

1 tbsp fresh marjoram
salt and pepper

1 Gently wipe each mushroom with a damp cloth to remove any excess dirt. Slice the mushrooms thinly, using a sharp knife.

2 Mix together the olive oil and lemon juice and pour the mixture over the mushrooms. Toss together so that the mushrooms are completely coated with the lemon juice and oil.

3 Stir the chopped anchovy fillets into the mushrooms. Season the mushroom mixture with black pepper and garnish with the fresh marjoram.

4 Leave the mushroom salad to stand for 5 minutes before serving in order for all the flavours to be absorbed. Season with a little salt (see Cook's Tip, below) and then serve.

COOK'S TIP

Do not season the mushroom salad with salt until the very last minute as it will cause the mushrooms to blacken and the juices to leak. The result will not be as tasty as it should be as the full flavours won't be absorbed and it will also look very unattractive.

COOK'S TIP

If you use dried herbs rather than fresh, remember that you need only about one third of dried to fresh.

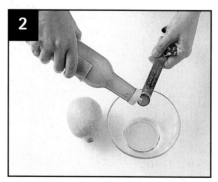

Yellow (Bell) Pepper Salad

A colourful combination of yellow (bell) peppers, red radishes and celery combine to give a wonderfully crunchy texture and fresh taste.

Serves 4

INGREDIENTS

4 rashers streaky bacon, chopped
2 yellow (bell) peppers
8 radishes, washed and trimmed

1 stick celery, finely chopped
3 plum tomatoes, cut into wedges
3 tbsp olive oil

1 tbsp fresh thyme

1 Dry fry the chopped bacon in a frying pan (skillet) for 4–5 minutes or until crispy. Remove the bacon from the frying pan (skillet), set aside and leave to cool until required.

2 Using a sharp knife, halve and deseed the (bell) peppers. Slice the (bell) peppers into long strips.

3 Using a sharp knife, halve the radishes and cut them into wedges.

4 Mix together the (bell) peppers, radishes, celery and tomatoes and toss the mixture in the olive oil and fresh thyme. Season to taste with a little salt and pepper.

5 Transfer the salad to serving plates and garnish with the reserved crispy bacon.

COOK'S TIP

Tomatoes are actually berries and are related to potatoes. There are many different shapes and sizes of this versatile fruit. The one most used in Italian cooking is the plum tomato which is very flavoursome.

COOK'S TIP

Pre-packaged diced bacon can be purchased from most supermarkets, which helps to save on preparation time.

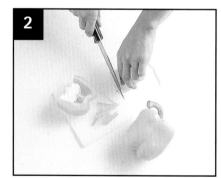

Spinach Salad

Fresh baby spinach is tasty and light, and it makes an excellent salad to go with the chicken and creamy dressing.

Serves 4

INGREDIENTS

100 g/3 1/2 oz baby spinach, washed
75 g/2 3/4 oz radicchio leaves,
   shredded
50 g/1 3/4 oz mushrooms

100 g/3 1/2 oz cooked chicken,
   preferably breast
50 g/1 3/4 oz Parma ham (prosciutto)
2 tbsp olive oil

finely grated rind of 1/2 orange and
   juice of 1 orange
1 tbsp natural yogurt

1 Wipe the mushrooms with a damp cloth to remove any excess dirt.

2 Gently mix together the spinach and radicchio in a large salad bowl.

3 Thinly slice the wiped mushrooms and add them to the bowl containing the spinach and radicchio.

4 Tear the cooked chicken breast and Parma ham (prosciutto) into strips and mix them into the salad.

5 To make the dressing, place the olive oil, orange rind, juice and yogurt into a screw-top jar. Shake the jar until the mixture is well combined. Season to taste with salt and pepper.

6 Drizzle the dressing over the spinach salad and toss to mix well. Serve immediately.

COOK'S TIP

Radiccio is a variety of chicory (endive) originating in Italy. It has a slightly bitter flavour.

VARIATION

Spinach is delicious when served raw. Try raw spinach in a salad garnished with bacon or garlicky croûtons. The young leaves have a wonderfully sharp flavour.

Sweet & Sour Aubergine (Eggplant) Salad

This cooked salad from Sicily was first brought to Italy by the Moors.

Serves 4

INGREDIENTS

6 tbsp olive oil
1 onion, chopped
2 garlic cloves, chopped
2 sticks celery, chopped
450 g/1 lb aubergines (eggplant)

1 x 400 g/14 oz can tomatoes, chopped
50 g/1³/₄ oz green olives, stoned and chopped
25 g/1 oz granulated sugar

100 ml/3¹/₂ fl oz/2¹/₃ cup red wine vinegar
25 g/1 oz capers, drained
salt and pepper
1 tbsp flat leaf parsley, roughly chopped, to garnish

1 Heat 2 tablespoons of the oil in a large frying pan (skillet). Add the prepared onions, garlic and celery to the frying pan (skillet) and cook, stirring, for 3–4 minutes.

2 Using a sharp knife, slice the aubergines (eggplants) into thick rounds, then cut each round into 4 pieces.

3 Add the aubergine (eggplant) pieces to the frying pan (skillet) with the remaining olive oil and fry for 5 minutes or until golden.

4 Add the tomatoes, olives and sugar to the pan, stirring until the sugar has dissolved.

5 Add the red wine vinegar, reduce the heat and leave to simmer for 10–15 minutes or until the sauce is thick and the aubergines (eggplants) are tender.

6 While the pan is still on the heat, stir in the capers. Season to taste with salt and pepper.

7 Transfer to serving plates and garnish with the chopped fresh parsley.

COOK'S TIP

This salad is best served cold the day after it is made, which allows the flavours to mingle and be fully absorbed.

Lentil & Tuna Salad

In this recipe, lentils, combined with spices, lemon juice and tuna, make a wonderfully tasty and filling salad.

Serves 4

INGREDIENTS

3 tbsp virgin olive oil
1 tbsp lemon juice
1 tsp wholegrain mustard
1 garlic clove, crushed

$1/2$ tsp cumin powder
$1/2$ tsp ground coriander
1 small red onion
2 ripe tomatoes
1 x 400 g/14 oz can lentils, drained

1 x 185 g/$6^{1/2}$ can tuna, drained
2 tbsp fresh coriander (cilantro), chopped
pepper

1 Using a sharp knife, deseed the tomatoes and chop them into fine dice.

2 Using a sharp knife, finely chop the red onion.

3 To make the dressing, whisk together the virgin olive oil, lemon juice, mustard, garlic, cumin powder and ground coriander in a small bowl. Set aside until required.

4 Mix together the chopped onion, diced tomatoes and drained lentils in a large bowl.

5 Flake the tuna and stir it into the onion, tomato and lentil mix.ture.

6 Stir in the chopped fresh coriander (cilantro).

7 Pour the dressing over the lentil and tuna salad and season with freshly ground black pepper. Serve at once.

VARIATION

Nuts would add extra flavour and texture to this salad.

COOK'S TIP

Lentils are a good source of protein and contain important vitamins and minerals. Buy them dried for soaking and cooking yourself, or buy canned varieties for speed and convenience.

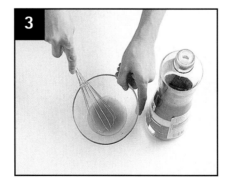

Bruschetta with Tomatoes

*Using ripe tomatoes and the best olive oil will
make this Tuscan dish absolutely delicious.*

Serves 4

INGREDIENTS

300 g/10 1/2 oz cherry tomatoes

4 sun-dried tomatoes

4 tbsp extra virgin olive oil

16 fresh basil leaves, shredded

8 slices ciabatta

2 garlic cloves, peeled

salt and pepper

1 Using a sharp knife, cut the cherry tomatoes in half.

2 Using a sharp knife, slice the sun-dried tomatoes into strips.

3 Place the cherry tomatoes and sun-dried tomatoes in a bowl. Add the olive oil and the shredded basil leaves and toss to mix well. Season to taste with a little salt and pepper.

4 Using a sharp knife, cut the garlic cloves in half. Lightly toast the ciabatta bread.

5 Rub the garlic, cut-side down, over both sides of the toasted ciabatta bread.

6 Top the ciabatta bread with the tomato mixture and serve immediately.

COOK'S TIP

Ciabatta is an Italian rustic bread which is slightly holey and quite chewy. It is very good in this recipe as it absorbs the full flavour of the garlic and extra virgin olive oil.

VARIATION

Plum tomatoes are also good in this recipe. Halve them, then cut them into wedges. Mix them with the sun-dried tomatoes in step 3.

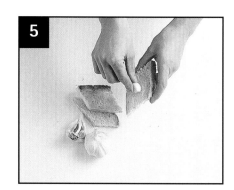

Italian Omelette

A baked omelette of substantial proportions with potatoes, onions, artichokes and sun-dried tomatoes.

Serves 4

INGREDIENTS

900 g/2 lb potatoes
1 tbsp oil
1 large onions, sliced
2 garlic cloves, chopped

6 sun-dried tomatoes, cut into strips
1 x 400g/14 oz can artichoke hearts, drained and halved
250 g/9 oz ricotta cheese

4 large eggs, beaten
2 tbsp milk
50 g/1^3/$_4$ oz Parmesan cheese, grated
3 tbsp chopped thyme

1 Peel the potatoes and place them in a bowl of cold water (see Cook's Tip). Cut the potatoes into thin slices.

2 Bring a large pan of water to the boil and add the potato slices. Leave the potatoes to simmer for 5–6 minutes or until just tender.

3 Heat the oil in a large frying pan (skillet). Add the onions and garlic to the pan and cook, stirring occasionally, for about 3–4 minutes.

4 Add the sun-dried tomatoes and continue cooking for a further 2 minutes.

5 Place a layer of potatoes at the bottom of a deep, ovenproof dish. Top with a layer of the onion mixture, artichokes and ricotta cheese. Repeat the layers in the same order, finishing with a layer of potatoes on top.

6 Beat the eggs, milk, half of the Parmesan, thyme and salt and pepper to taste together and pour over the potatoes.

7 Top with the remaining Parmesan cheese and bake in a preheated oven, at 190°C/375°F/ Gas Mark 5, for 20–25 minutes or until golden brown. Cut into slices and serve.

COOK'S TIP

Placing the potatoes in a bowl of cold water will prevent them from turning brown while you cut the rest into slices.

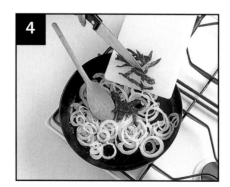

Casserole of Beans in Tomato Sauce

*This quick and easy casserole can be eaten as a healthy
supper dish or as a side dish to accompany sausages or grilled fish.*

Serves 4

INGREDIENTS

1 x 400g/14 oz can cannellini beans
1 x 400g/14 oz can borlotti beans
2 tbsp olive oil

1 stick celery
2 garlic cloves, chopped
175 g/6 oz baby onions, halved

450 g/1 lb tomatoes
75 g/2 3/4 oz rocket (arugula)

1 Drain both cans of beans and reserve 6 tbsp of the liquid.

2 Heat the oil in a large pan. Add the celery, garlic and onions and sauté for 5 minutes or until the onions are golden.

3 Cut a cross in the base of each tomato and plunge them into a bowl of boiling water for 30 seconds until the skins split. Remove them with a perforated spoon and leave until cool enough to handle. Peel off the skin and chop the flesh. Add the tomato flesh and the reserved bean liquid to the pan and cook for 5 minutes.

4 Add the beans to the pan and cook for a further 3–4 minutes or until the beans are hot.

5 Stir in the rocket (arugula) and allow to wilt slightly before serving.

COOK'S TIP

Another way to peel tomatoes is once you have cut a cross in the base, push it on to a fork and hold it over a gas flame, turning it slowly so that the skin heats evenly all over. The skin will start to bubble and split, and should then slide off easily.

VARIATION

For a spicier tasting dish, add 1–2 teaspoons of hot pepper sauce with the beans in step 4.

Small Pancakes with Smoked Fish

*These are delicious as a starter or light supper dish and
you can vary the filling with whichever fish you prefer.*

Makes 12 pancakes

INGREDIENTS

PANCAKES:
100 g/3^1/$_2$ oz flour
^{1}/$_2$ tsp salt
1 egg, beaten
300 ml/^{1}/$_2$ pint/1^1/$_4$ cups milk
1 tbsp oil, for frying

SAUCE:
450 g/1lb smoked haddock, skinned
300 ml/^{1}/$_2$ pint/1^1/$_4$ cups milk
40 g/1^1/$_2$ oz/3 tbsp butter or
  margarine
40 g/1^1/$_2$ oz flour
300 ml/^{1}/$_2$ pint/1^1/$_4$ cups fish stock

75 g/2^3/$_4$ oz Parmesan cheese, grated
100 g/3^1/$_2$ oz peas, frozen and
  defrosted
100 g/3^1/$_2$ oz prawns (shrimp),
  cooked and peeled
50 g/1^3/$_4$ oz Gruyère cheese, grated
salt and pepper

1 To make the pancake batter, sift the flour and salt into a large bowl and make a well in the centre. Add the egg and, using a wooden spoon, begin to draw in the flour. Slowly add the milk and beat to form a smooth batter. Set aside until required.

2 Place the fish in a large frying pan (skillet), add the milk and bring to the boil. Simmer for 10 minutes or until the fish begins to flake. Drain, reserving the milk.

3 Melt the butter in a saucepan. Add the flour, mix to a paste and cook for 2–3 minutes. Remove the pan from the heat and add the reserved milk a little at a time, stirring to make a smooth sauce. Repeat with the fish stock. Return to the heat and bring to the boil, stirring. Stir in the Parmesan and season with salt and pepper.

4 Grease a frying pan (skillet) with oil. Add 2 tablespoons of the pancake batter, swirling it

round and cook for 2–3 minutes. Loosen the sides with a palette knife (spatula) and flip over the pancake. Cook for 2–3 minutes until golden; repeat. Stack the pancakes with sheets of baking parchment between them and keep warm in the oven.

5 Stir the flaked fish, peas and prawns (shrimp) into half of the sauce and use to fill each pancake. Pour over the remaining sauce, top with the Gruyère and bake for 20 minutes until golden.

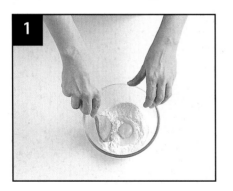

Roasted Seafood

Vegetables become deliciously sweet and juicy when they are roasted, and they go particularly well with fish and seafood.

Serves 4

INGREDIENTS

600 g/1lb 5oz new potatoes

3 red onions, cut into wedges

2 courgettes (zucchini), sliced into chunks

8 garlic cloves, peeled

2 lemons, cut into wedges

4 sprigs rosemary

4 tbsp olive oil

350 g/12oz shell-on prawns (shrimp), preferably uncooked

2 small squid, chopped into rings

4 tomatoes, quartered

1 Scrub the potatoes to remove any excess dirt. Cut any large potatoes in half. Place the potatoes in a large roasting tin (pan), together with the onions, courgettes (zucchini), garlic, lemon and rosemary.

2 Pour over the oil and toss to coat all of the vegetables in the oil.

3 Cook in a preheated oven, at 200°C/400°F/Gas Mark 6, for about 40 minutes, turning occasionally, until the potatoes are tender.

4 Once the potatoes are tender, add the prawns (shrimp), squid and tomatoes, tossing to coat them in the oil, and roast for 10 minutes. All of the vegetables should be cooked through and slightly charred for full flavour.

5 Transfer to serving plates and serve hot.

COOK'S TIP

Squid and octopus are great favourites in Italy and all around the Mediterranean.

VARIATION

Most vegetables are suitable for roasting in the oven. Try adding 450 g/ 1 lb pumpkin, squash or aubergine (eggplant), if you prefer.

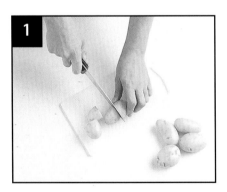

Omelette Strips in Tomato Sauce

These omelette strips are delicious smothered in tomato sauce.

Serves 4

INGREDIENTS

25 g/1 oz/2 tbsp butter
1 onion, finely chopped
2 garlic cloves, chopped
4 eggs, beaten

150 ml/5 fl oz/^{2}/$_3$ cup milk
75 g/2 ^{3}/$_4$ oz Gruyère cheese, diced
1 x 400g/14 oz can tomatoes,
   chopped

1 tbsp rosemary, stalks removed
150 ml/5 fl oz/^{2}/$_3$ cup vegetable stock
freshly grated Parmesan cheese, for
   sprinkling
crusty bread, to serve

1 Melt the butter in a large frying pan (skillet). Add the onion and garlic and cook for 4–5 minutes, until softened.

2 Beat together the eggs and milk and add the mixture to the frying pan (skillet).

3 Using a spatula, gently raise the cooked edges of the omelette and tip any uncooked egg around the edge of the pan.

4 Scatter over the cheese. Cook for 5 minutes, turning once, until golden on both sides. Remove from the pan and roll up.

5 Add the tomatoes, rosemary and vegetable stock to the frying pan (skillet), stirring, and bring to the boil.

6 Leave the tomato sauce to simmer for about 10 minutes until reduced and thickened.

7 Slice the omelette into strips and add to the tomato sauce in the frying pan (skillet). Cook for 3–4 minutes until piping hot.

8 Sprinkle the freshly grated Parmesan cheese over the omelette strips in tomato sauce and serve with fresh crusty bread.

VARIATION

Try adding 100 g/ 3^1/$_2$ oz diced pancetta or unsmoked bacon in step 1 and cooking the meat with the onions .

Mozzarella in Carriages

These deep-fried Mozzarella sandwiches are a tasty snack at any time of the day, or serve smaller triangles as an antipasto with drinks.

Serves 4

INGREDIENTS

8 slices bread, preferably slightly
   stale, crusts removed
100 g/3^1/$_2$ oz Mozzarella cheese,
   sliced thickly

8 canned anchovy fillets, drained and
   chopped
16 fresh basil leaves
50 g/1^3/$_4$ oz black olives, chopped

4 eggs, beaten
150 ml/5 floz/^{2}/$_3$ cup milk
oil, for deep-frying
salt and pepper

1 Cut each slice of bread into 2 triangles. Top 8 of the bread triangles with the Mozzarella slices and chopped anchovies.

2 Place the basil leaves and olives on top and season with salt and pepper to taste.

3 Lay the other 8 triangles of bread over the top and press down round the edges to seal.

4 Mix the eggs and milk and pour into an ovenproof dish. Add the sandwiches and leave to soak for 5 minutes.

5 Heat the oil in a large saucepan to 180°–190°C/350°–375°F or until a cube of bread browns in 30 seconds.

6 Before cooking the sandwiches, squeeze the edges together again.

7 Carefully place the sandwiches in the oil and deep-fry for 2 minutes or until golden, turning once. Remove the sandwiches with a perforated spoon and drain on absorbent kitchen paper. Serve immediately while still hot.

COOK'S TIP

If you prefer, try adding a peeled prawn (shrimp) to each triangle. For smaller sandwiches, cut the bread into 4 triangles.

Baked Fennel

Fennel is used a lot in northern Italy. It is a very versatile
vegetable, which is good cooked or in salads.

Serves 4

INGREDIENTS
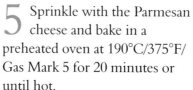

2 fennel bulbs
2 celery sticks cut into 7.5 cm/3 inch
sticks

6 sun-dried tomatoes, halved
200 g/7 oz passata (tomato paste)

2 tsp dried oregano
50 g/1³/4 oz Parmesan cheese, grated

1 Using a sharp knife, trim the fennel, discarding any tough outer leaves, and cut the bulb into quarters.

2 Bring a large pan of water to the boil, add the fennel and celery and cook for 8–10 minutes or until just tender. Remove with a perforated spoon and drain.

3 Place the fennel pieces, celery and sun-dried tomatoes in an ovenproof dish.

4 Mix the passata (tomato paste) and oregano and pour the mixture over the fennel.

5 Sprinkle with the Parmesan cheese and bake in a preheated oven at 190°C/375°F/ Gas Mark 5 for 20 minutes or until hot.

6 Serve as a starter with bread or as a vegetable side dish.

VARIATION

If you cannot find any fennel in the shops, leeks make a delicious alternative. Use about 750 g/1 lb 10 oz, chopped, making sure that they are washed thoroughly to remove all traces of soil.

VARIATION

Add 1 x 400 g/14 oz can butter beans, drained, in step 3 for a substantial vegetarian supper dish.

Garlic & Pine Nut Tarts

*A crisp lining of bread is filled with garlic butter
and pine nuts to make a delightful starter.*

Serves 4

INGREDIENTS

4 slices wholemeal or granary bread
50 g/1³/₄ oz pine nuts
150 g/5¹/₂ oz/10 tbsp butter

5 garlic cloves, peeled and halved
2 tbsp fresh oregano, chopped, plus
extra for garnish

4 black olives, halved
oregano leaves, to garnish

1 Using a rolling pin, flatten the bread slightly. Using a pastry cutter, cut out 4 circles to fit your individual tart tins – they should measure about 10 cm/ 4 inches across. Reserve the offcuts of bread and leave them in the refrigerator for 10 minutes or until required.

2 Meanwhile, place the pine nuts on a baking tray (cookie sheet). Toast the pine nuts under a preheated grill (broiler) for 2–3 minutes or until golden.

3 Put the bread offcuts, pine nuts, butter, garlic and oregano into a food processor and blend for about 20 seconds. Alternatively, pound the ingredients by hand in a mortar and pestle. The mixture should have a rough texture.

4 Spoon the pine nut butter mixture into the lined tin and top with the olives. Bake in a preheated oven at 200°C/400°F/ Gas Mark 6 for 10–15 minutes or until golden.

5 Transfer the tarts to serving plates and serve warm garnished with the fresh oregano leaves.

VARIATION

Puff pastry can be used instead of the bread for the tart cases. Use 200 g/7oz puff pastry to line 4 tart tins. Leave the puff pastry to chill in the refrigerator for 20 minutes. Line the tart tins with the pastry and foil and bake blind for 10 minutes. Remove the foil and bake for 3–4 minutes or until the pastry is just set. Leave to cool, then continue from step 2, adding 2 tablespoons of breadcrumbs to the mixture.

Potatoes with Olives & Anchovies

This side dish makes a delicious accompaniment for grilled fish or for lamb chops.
The fennel adds a subtle aniseed flavour.

Serves 4

INGREDIENTS

450 g/1lb baby new potatoes, scrubbed
2 tbsp olive oil

2 fennel bulbs, trimmed and sliced
2 sprigs rosemary, stalks removed
75 g/2³/4 oz mixed olives

8 canned anchovy fillets, drained and chopped

1 Bring a large saucepan of water to the boil and cook the potatoes for 8–10 minutes or until tender. Remove the potatoes from the saucepan using a perforated spoon and set aside to cool slightly.

2 Once the potatoes are just cool enough to handle, cut them into wedges, using a sharp knife.

3 Pit the mixed olives and cut them in half, using a sharp knife.

4 Using a sharp knife, chop the anchovy fillets into smaller strips.

5 Heat the oil in a large frying pan (skillet). Add the potato wedges, sliced fennel and rosemary. Cook for 7–8 minutes or until the potatoes are golden.

6 Stir in the olives and anchovies and cook for 1 minute or until warmed through.

7 Transfer to serving plates and serve immediately.

COOK'S TIP

Fresh rosemary is a particular favourite with Italians, but you can experiment with your favourite herbs in this recipe, if you prefer.

Tuscan Chicken Livers on Toast

Crostini are small pieces of toast with a savoury topping.
In Italy this is a popular antipasto dish.

Serves 4

INGREDIENTS

2 tbsp olive oil
1 garlic clove, finely chopped
225 g/8 oz fresh or frozen chicken
   livers

4 fresh sage leaves, finely chopped or
   1 tsp dried, crumbled sage
2 tbsp white wine
2 tbsp lemon juice

salt and pepper
4 slices ciabatta or other Italian
   bread
wedges of lemon, to garnish

1 Heat the olive oil in a frying pan (skillet) and cook the garlic for 1 minute.

2 Rinse and roughly chop the chicken livers, using a sharp knife.

3 Add the chicken liver to the frying pan (skillet) together with the white wine and lemon juice. Cook for 3–4 minutes or until the juices from the chicken liver run clear.

4 Stir in the sage and season to taste with salt and pepper.

5 Under a preheated grill (broiler), toast the bread for 2 minutes on both sides or until golden-brown.

6 Spoon the hot chicken livers on top of the toasted bread and serve garnished with a wedge of lemon.

COOK'S TIP

Overcooked liver is dry and tasteless. Cook the chopped liver for only 3–4 minutes – it should be soft and tender.

VARIATION

Another way to make crostini is to slice a crusty loaf or a French loaf into small rounds or squares. Heat the olive oil in a frying pan (skillet) and fry the slices of bread until golden brown and crisp on both sides. Remove the crostini from the pan with a perforated spoon and leave to drain on paper towels. Top with the chicken livers.

Onion & Mozzarella Tarts

These individual tarts are delicious hot or cold and are great for picnics.

Serves 4

INGREDIENTS

1 x 250g/9 oz packet puff pastry, defrosted if frozen

2 medium red onions, cut into thin wedges

1 red (bell) pepper, halved and deseeded

8 cherry tomatoes, halved

100g/3 ¾ oz Mozzarella cheese, cut into chunks

8 sprigs thyme

1 Roll out the pastry to make 4 x 7.5 cm/3 inch squares. Using a sharp knife, trim the edges of the pastry, reserving the trimmings. Leave the pastry to chill in the refrigerator for 30 minutes.

2 Place the pastry squares on a baking tray (cookie sheet). Brush a little water along each edge of the pastry squares and use the reserved pastry trimmings to make a rim around each tart.

3 Cut the red onions into wedges and halve and deseed the (bell) peppers.

4 Place the onions and (bell) pepper in a roasting tin (pan). Cook under a preheated grill (broiler) for 15 minutes or until charred.

5 Place the roasted (bell) pepper halves in a polythene bag and leave to sweat for 10 minutes. Peel off the skin from the (bell) peppers and cut the flesh into strips.

6 Line the pastry squares with squares of foil. Bake in a preheated oven at 200°C/400°F/Gas Mark 6 for 10 minutes. Remove the foil squares and bake for a further 5 minutes.

7 Place the onions, (bell) pepper strips, tomatoes and cheese in each tart and sprinkle with the fresh thyme.

8 Return to the oven for 15 minutes or until the pastry is golden. Serve hot.

Pasta & Rice

Easy to cook and easy on the purse, pasta is wonderfully versatile. It can be served with meat, fish or vegetable sauces, or baked in the oven. Some of the most popular and well-known pasta dishes are those that combine long strands of pasta cooked 'al dente', with a rich, hearty meat sauce, such as Spaghetti Bolognese which needs no introduction. Fish and seafood are irresistible combined with pasta and need only the briefest of cooking times. Pasta combined with vegetables provides inspiration for countless dishes which will please vegetarians and meat-eaters alike.

Rice dishes are very popular in the north of Italy – they are particularly fond of risottos. Milanese and other risottos are made with short-grain rice, the best of which is Arborio – this type of rice should be rinsed before using. An Italian risotto is far moister than pilau or other savoury rice dish, but it should not be soggy.

Gnocchi are made with maize flour, cornmeal (polenta), potatoes or semolina, often combined with spinach or some sort of cheese. Gnocchi resemble dumplings and are either poached or baked, and served with a sauce. Polenta is made with either cornmeal or polenta flour and can be served either as a soft porridge or a firmer cake which is then fried until crisp.

Tagliatelle with Garlic Butter

Pasta is not difficult to make yourself, just a little time consuming. The resulting pasta only takes a couple of minutes to cook and it tastes wonderful.

Serves 4

INGREDIENTS

450 g/1 lb strong white flour, plus extra for dredging
2 tsp salt

4 eggs, beaten
3 tbsp olive oil
75 g/2³/₄ oz/5 tbsp butter, melted

3 garlic cloves, finely chopped
2 tbsp chopped, fresh parsley
pepper

1 Sift the flour into a large bowl and stir in the salt.

2 Make a well in the middle of the dry ingredients and add the eggs and 2 tablespoons of oil. Using a wooden spoon, stir in the eggs, gradually drawing in the flour. After a few minutes the dough will be too stiff to use a spoon and you will need to use your fingers.

3 Once all of the flour has been incorporated, turn the dough out on to a floured surface and knead for about 5 minutes, until smooth and elastic. If you find the dough is too wet, add a little more flour and continue kneading. Cover with cling film (plastic wrap) and leave to rest for at least 15 minutes.

4 The basic dough is now ready; roll out the pasta thinly and create the pasta shapes required. This can be done by hand or using a pasta machine. Results from a machine are usually neater and thinner, but not necessarily better.

5 To make the tagliatelle by hand, fold the thinly rolled pasta sheets into 3 and cut out long, thin stips, about 1 cm/ ¹/₂ inch wide.

6 To cook, bring a large pan of water to the boil, add 1 tablespoon of oil and the pasta. It will take 2–3 minutes to cook, and the texture should have a slight bite to it. Drain thoroughly.

7 Mix together the butter, garlic and parsley. Stir into the pasta and serve immediately with plenty of black pepper.

COOK'S TIP

Generally allow about 150 g/ 5¹/₂ oz fresh pasta or about 100 g/3¹/₂ dried pasta per person.

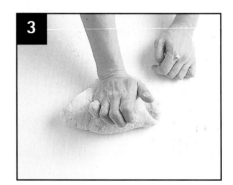

Spaghetti Bolognese

This classic dish is still a favourite in Bologna. The original recipe takes about 4 hours to cook and should be left over night to allow the flavours to mingle. This version is much quicker.

Serves 4

INGREDIENTS

1 tbsp olive oil
1 onion, finely chopped
2 garlic cloves, chopped
1 carrot, scraped and chopped
1 stick celery, chopped

50 g/1¾ oz pancetta or streaky
   bacon, diced
350 g/12 oz lean minced beef
1 x 400g/14 oz can chopped
   tomatoes

2 tsp dried oregano
125 ml/4 fl oz/scant ½ cup red wine
2 tbsp tomato purée
salt and pepper
675 g/1½ lb fresh spaghetti or
   350 g/12 oz dried spaghetti

1 Heat the oil in a large frying pan (skillet). Add the onions and cook for 3 minutes.

2 Add the garlic, carrot, celery and pancetta or bacon and sauté for 3–4 minutes or until just beginning to brown.

3 Add the beef and cook over a high heat for another 3 minutes or until all of the meat is brown.

4 Stir in the tomatoes, oregano and red wine and bring to the boil. Reduce the heat and leave to simmer for about 45 minutes.

5 Stir in the tomato purée and season with salt and pepper .

6 Cook the spaghetti in a pan of boiling water according to the instructions on the packet or until it is cooked, but still has 'bite'. Drain thoroughly.

7 Transfer the spaghetti to a serving plate and pour over the bolognese sauce. Toss to mix well and serve hot.

VARIATION

Try adding 25 g/1oz dried porcini, soaked for 10 minutes in 2 tablespoons of warm water, to the bolognese sauce in step 4, if you wish.

COOK'S TIP

The sauce can be stored in the freezer for 2 months or in the refrigerator for 2–3 days.

Spicy Tomato Tagliatelle

A deliciously fresh and slightly spicy tomato sauce which is excellent for lunch or a light supper.

Serves 4

INGREDIENTS

50 g/1³/₄ oz/3 tbsp butter
1 onion, finely chopped
1 garlic clove, crushed
2 small red chillies, deseeded and
   diced

450 g/1 lb fresh tomatoes, skinned,
   deseeded and diced
200 ml/7 fl oz/³/₄ cup vegetable stock
2 tbsp tomato purée
1 tsp sugar

salt and pepper
675 g/1¹/₂ lb fresh green and white
   tagliatelle, or 350 g/12 oz dried

---

1 Melt the butter in a large saucepan. Add the onion and garlic and cook for 3–4 minutes or until softened.

2 Add the chillies to the pan and continue cooking for about 2 minutes.

3 Add the tomatoes and stock, reduce the heat and leave to simmer for 10 minutes, stirring.

4 Pour the sauce into a food processor and blend for 1 minute until smooth.

Alternatively, push the sauce through a sieve.

5 Return the sauce to the pan and add the tomato purée, sugar, and salt and pepper to taste. Gently reheat over a low heat, until piping hot.

6 Cook the tagliatelle in a pan of boiling water according to the instructions on the packet or until it is cooked, but still has 'bite'. Drain the tagliatelle, transfer to serving plates and serve with the tomato sauce.

VARIATION

Try topping your pasta dish with 50 g/1³/₄ oz pancetta or unsmoked bacon, diced and dry-fried for 5 minutes until crispy.

Basil & Tomato Pasta

Roasting the tomatoes gives a sweeter and smoother flavour to this sauce. Try to buy Italian tomatoes, such as plum or flavia, as these have a better flavour and colour.

Serves 4

INGREDIENTS

1 tbsp olive oil
2 sprigs rosemary
2 cloves garlic, unpeeled

450 g/1 lb tomatoes, halved
1 tbsp sun-dried tomato paste
12 fresh basil leaves, plus extra to garnish

salt and pepper
675 g/1^1/$_2$ lb fresh farfalle or 350 g/12 oz dried farfalle

1 Place the oil, rosemary, garlic and tomatoes, skin side up, in a shallow roasting tin (pan).

2 Drizzle with a little oil and cook under a preheated grill (broiler) for 20 minutes or until the tomato skins are slightly charred.

3 Peel the skin from the tomatoes. Roughly chop the tomato flesh and place in a pan.

4 Squeeze the pulp from the garlic cloves and mix with the tomato flesh and sun-dried tomato paste.

5 Roughly tear the fresh basil leaves into smaller pieces and then stir them into the sauce. Season with a little salt and pepper to taste.

6 Cook the farfalle in a saucepan of boiling water according to the instructions on the packet or until it is cooked through, but still has 'bite'. Drain.

7 Gently heat the tomato and basil sauce.

8 Transfer the farfalle to serving plates and serve with the basil and tomato sauce.

COOK'S TIP

This sauce tastes just as good when served cold in a pasta salad.

Pasta Vongole

Fresh clams are available from most good fishmongers. If you prefer, used canned clams, which are less messy to eat but not so pretty to serve.

Serves 4

INGREDIENTS

675 g/1¹/₂ lb fresh clams or 1 x
   290 g/10 oz can clams, drained
400 g/14 oz mixed seafood, such as
   prawns (shrimps), squid and
   mussels, defrosted if frozen

2 tbsp olive oil
2 cloves garlic, finely chopped
150 ml/5 fl oz/²/₃ cup white wine
150 ml/5 fl oz/²/₃ cup fish stock
2 tbsp chopped tarragon

salt and pepper
675 g/1¹/₂ lb fresh pasta or
   350 g/12 oz dried pasta

1 If you are using fresh clams, scrub them clean and discard any that are already open.

2 Heat the oil in a large frying pan (skillet). Add the garlic and the clams to the pan and cook for 2 minutes, shaking the pan to ensure that all of the clams are coated in the oil.

3 Add the remaining seafood mixture to the pan and cook for a further 2 minutes.

4 Pour the wine and stock over the mixed seafood and garlic and bring to the boil. Cover the pan, reduce the heat and leave to simmer for 8–10 minutes or until the shells open. Discard any clams or mussels that do not open.

5 Meanwhile, cook the pasta in a saucepan of boiling water according to the instructions on the packet or until it is cooked through, but still has 'bite'. Drain.

6 Stir the tarragon into the sauce and season to taste.

7 Transfer the pasta to a serving plate and pour over the sauce.

VARIATION

Red clam sauce can be made by adding 8 tablespoons of passata (tomato purée) to the sauce along with the stock in step 4. Follow the same cooking method.

Basil & Pine Nut Pesto

Delicious stirred into pasta, soups and salad dressings, pesto is available in most supermarkets, but making your own gives a much fresher, fuller flavour.

Serves 4

INGREDIENTS

about 40 fresh basil leaves, washed and dried
3 garlic cloves, crushed
25 g/1 oz pine nuts

50 g/1 3/4 oz Parmesan cheese, finely grated
2–3 tbsp extra virgin olive oil
salt and pepper

675 g/1 1/2 lb fresh pasta or
350 g/12 oz dried pasta

1 Rinse the basil leaves and pat them dry with paper towels.

2 Put the basil leaves, garlic, pine nuts and grated Parmesan into a food processor and blend for about 30 seconds or until smooth. Alternatively, pound the ingredients by hand, using a mortar and pestle.

3 If you are using a food processor, keep the motor running and slowly add the olive oil. Alternatively, add the oil drop by drop while stirring briskly. Season with salt and pepper.

4 Meanwhile, cook the pasta in a saucepan of boiling water according to the instructions on the packet or until it is cooked through, but still has 'bite'. Drain.

5 Transfer the pasta to a serving plate and serve with the pesto. Toss to mix well and serve hot.

VARIATION

Try making a walnut version of this pesto. Substitute 25 g/1 oz walnuts for the pine nuts and add 1 tablespoon walnut oil in step 2.

COOK'S TIP

You can store pesto in the refrigerator for about 4 weeks. Cover the surface of the pesto with olive oil before sealing the container or bottle, to prevent the basil from oxidising and turning black.

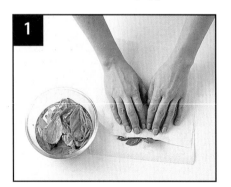

Chilli & (Bell) Pepper Pasta Salad

This roasted (bell) pepper and chilli sauce is sweet and spicy.

Serves 4

INGREDIENTS

2 red (bell) peppers, halved and
   deseeded
1 small red chilli
2 garlic cloves

4 tomatoes, halved
50 g/1 $^{3}/_{4}$ oz ground almonds
7 tbsp olive oil

675 g/1 $^{1}/_{2}$ lb fresh pasta or
   350 g/12 oz dried pasta
fresh oregano leaves, to garnish

1 Place the (bell) peppers, skin-side up, on a baking tray (cookie sheet) with the chilli and garlic. Cook under a preheated grill (broiler) for 15 minutes or until charred. After 10 minutes turn the tomatoes skin-side up.

2 Place the (bell) peppers and chillies in a polythene bag and leave to sweat for 10 minutes.

3 Remove the skin from the (bell) peppers and chillies and slice the flesh into strips, using a sharp knife.

4 Peel the garlic and peel and deseed the tomatoes.

5 Place the almonds on a baking tray (cookie sheet) and place under the grill (broiler) for 2–3 minutes until golden.

6 Using a food processor, blend the (bell) pepper, chilli, garlic and tomatoes to make a purée. Keep the motor running and slowly add the olive oil to form a thick sauce. Alternatively, mash the mixture with a fork and beat in the olive oil, drop by drop.

7 Stir the toasted ground almonds into the mixture.

8 Warm the sauce in a saucepan until it is heated through.

9 Cook the pasta in a saucepan of boiling water according to the instructions on the packet or until it is cooked through, but still has 'bite'. Drain the pasta and transfer to a serving dish. Pour over the sauce and toss to mix. Garnish with fresh oregano leaves.

VARIATION

Add 2 tablespoons of red wine vinegar to the sauce and use as a dressing for a cold pasta salad, if you wish.

Pasta Carbonara

Lightly cooked eggs and pancetta are combined with cheese to make this rich, classic sauce.

Serves 4

INGREDIENTS

1 tbsp olive oil
40 g/1¹/₂ oz/3 tbsp butter
100 g/3¹/₂ oz pancetta or unsmoked
   bacon, diced

3 eggs, beaten
2 tbsp milk
1 tbsp thyme, stalks removed
675 g/1¹/₂ lb fresh or 350 g/12 oz
   dried conchigoni rigati

salt and pepper
50 g/1³/₄ oz Parmesan cheese, grated

1 Heat the oil and butter in a frying pan (skillet) until the mixture is just beginning to froth.

2 Add the pancetta or bacon to the pan and cook for 5 minutes or until browned all over.

3 Mix together the eggs and milk in a small bowl. Stir in the thyme and season to taste with salt and pepper.

4 Cook the pasta in a saucepan of boiling water according to the instructions on the packet or until it is cooked through, but still has 'bite'. Drain thoroughly.

5 Add the cooked, drained pasta to the frying pan (skillet) with the eggs and cook over a high heat for about 30 seconds until the eggs just begin to cook and set. Do not overcook the eggs or they will become rubbery.

6 Stir in half of the grated Parmesan cheese.

7 Transfer the pasta to a serving plate, pour over the sauce and toss to mix well.

8 Sprinkle the rest of the grated Parmesan over the top and serve immediately.

VARIATION

For an extra rich carbonara sauce, stir in 4 tablespoons of double (heavy) cream with the eggs and milk in step 3. Follow exactly the same cooking method.

Pasta & Sicilian Sauce

This Sicilian recipe of anchovies mixed with pine nuts
and sultanas in a tomato sauce is delicious with all types of pasta.

Serves 4

INGREDIENTS

450 g/1lb tomatoes, halved
25 g/1 oz pine nuts
50 g/1³/₄ oz sultanas

1 x 50 g/1³/₄ oz can anchovies,
  drained and halved lengthways
2 tbsp concentrated tomato purée

675 g/1¹/₂ lb fresh or 350 g/12 oz
  dried penne

1 Cook the tomatoes under a preheated grill (broiler) for about 10 minutes. Leave to cool slightly, then once cool enough to handle, peel off the skin and dice the flesh.

2 Place the pine nuts on a baking tray (cookie sheet) and lightly toast under the grill (broiler) for 2–3 minutes or until golden.

3 Soak the sultanas in a bowl of warm water for about 20 minutes. Drain the sultanas thoroughly.

4 Place the tomatoes, pine nuts and sultanas in a small pan and gently heat.

5 Add the anchovies and tomato purée, heating the sauce for a further 2–3 minutes or until hot.

6 Cook the pasta in a saucepan of boiling water according to the instructions on the packet or until it is cooked through, but still has 'bite'. Drain thoroughly.

7 Transfer the pasta to a serving plate and serve with the hot Sicilian sauce.

VARIATION

Add 100 g/3¹/₂ oz bacon, grilled
for 5 minutes until crispy, then
chopped, instead of the
anchovies, if you prefer.

COOK'S TIP

If you are making fresh pasta (see
page 100), remember that pasta
dough prefers warm conditions and
responds well to handling. Do not
leave to chill and do not use a
marble surface for kneading.

Chicken Lasagne

This variation of the traditional beef dish has layers of pasta and chicken or turkey baked in red wine, tomatoes and a delicious cheese sauce.

Serves 4

INGREDIENTS

350 g/12 oz fresh lasagne (about 9 sheets) or 150 g/5¹/₂ oz dried lasagne (about 9 sheets)
1 tbsp olive oil
1 red onion, finely chopped
1 garlic clove, crushed
100 g/3¹/₂ oz mushrooms, wiped and sliced

350 g/12 oz chicken or turkey breast, cut into chunks
150 ml/5 fl oz/²/₃ cup red wine, diluted with 100 ml/3¹/₂ fl oz/scant ¹/₃ cup water
250 g/9 oz passata (tomato purée)
1 tsp sugar

BÉCHAMEL SAUCE:
75 g/2³/₄ oz/5 tbsp butter
50 g/1³/₄ oz plain (all-purpose) flour
600 ml/1 pint/2¹/₂ cups milk
1 egg, beaten
75 g/2³/₄ oz Parmesan cheese, grated
salt and pepper

1 Cook the lasagne in a pan of boiling water according to the instructions on the packet. Lightly grease a deep ovenproof dish.

2 Heat the oil in a pan. Add the onion and garlic and cook for 3–4 minutes. Add the mushrooms and chicken and stir-fry for 4 minutes or until the meat browns.

3 Add the wine, bring to the boil, then leave to simmer for 5 minutes. Stir in the passata (tomato purée) and sugar and cook for 3–5 minutes until the meat is tender and cooked through. The sauce should have thickened but still be quite runny.

4 To make the béchamel sauce, melt the butter in a pan, stir in the flour and cook for 2 minutes. Remove the pan from the heat and gradually add the milk, mixing to form a smooth sauce. Return the pan to the heat and bring to the boil, stirring until thickened. Leave to cool slightly, then beat in the egg and half of the cheese. Season to taste.

5 Place 3 sheets of lasagne in the base of the dish and spread with half of the chicken mixture. Repeat the layers. Top with the last 3 sheets of lasagne, pour over the Béchamel sauce and sprinkle with the Parmesan. Bake in a preheated oven at 190°C/375°F/ Gas Mark 5 for 30 minutes until golden and the pasta is cooked.

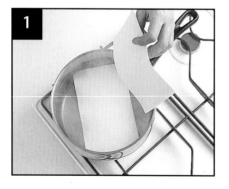

Cannelloni

It is easier to use dried pasta in this recipe – you can buy it ready made in tubes.
If you are using fresh pasta (see page 100), you must cut out squares and roll them yourself.

Serves 4

INGREDIENTS

20 tubes dried cannelloni (about
   200 g/7 oz) or 20 square sheets of
   fresh pasta (about 350 g/12 oz)
250 g/9 oz ricotta cheese
150 g/5$\frac{1}{2}$ oz frozen spinach,
   defrosted

$\frac{1}{2}$ small red (bell) pepper, diced
2 spring onions (scallions), chopped
150 ml/5 fl oz/$\frac{2}{3}$ cup hot vegetable
   or chicken stock

1 portion of Basil and Tomato Sauce
   (see page 106)
5 g/1 oz Parmesan or pecorino
   cheese, grated
salt and pepper

1 If you are using dried cannelloni, check the packet instructions; many varieties do not need pre-cooking. If necessary, pre-cook your pasta. Bring a large saucepan of water to the boil, add 1 tablespoon of oil and cook the pasta for 3–4 minutes – it is easier to do this in batches.

2 In a bowl, mix together the ricotta, spinach, (bell) pepper, and spring onions (scallions) and season to taste with salt and pepper.

3 Lightly butter an ovenproof dish, large enough to contain all of the pasta tubes in a single layer. Spoon the ricotta mixture into the pasta tubes and place them into the prepared dish. If you are using fresh sheets of pasta, spread the ricotta mixture along one side of each fresh pasta square and roll up to form a tube.

4 Mix together the stock and Basil and Tomato Sauce (see page 106) and pour over the pasta tubes.

5 Sprinkle the cheese over the cannelloni and bake in a preheated oven, 190°C/375°F/Gas Mark 5, for 20–25 minutes or until the pasta is cooked through.

VARIATION

If you would prefer a creamier version, omit the stock and the Basil and Tomato sauce and replace with Béchamel Sauce (see page 118).

Tortelloni

These tasty little squares of pasta stuffed with mushrooms and cheese are surprisingly filling. Serve about 3 pieces for a starter and up to 9 for a main course.

Makes 36 pieces

INGREDIENTS

about 300 g/10^{1}/$_2$ oz fresh pasta (see page 100), rolled out to thin sheets
75 g/2^{3}/$_4$ oz/5 tbsp butter
50 g/1^{3}/$_4$ oz shallots, finely chopped

3 garlic clove, crushed
50 g/1^{3}/$_4$ oz mushrooms, wiped and finely chopped
^{1}/$_2$ stick celery, finely chopped

25 g/1 oz pecorino cheese, finely grated, plus extra to garnish
1 tbsp oil
salt and pepper

1 Using a serrated pasta cutter, cut 5 cm/2 inch squares from the sheets of fresh pasta. To make 36 tortelloni you will need 72 squares. Once the pasta is cut, cover the squares with cling film (plastic wrap) to stop them drying out.

2 Heat 25 g/1 oz/3 tbsp of the butter in a frying pan (skillet). Add the shallots, 1 crushed garlic clove, the mushrooms and celery and cook for 4–5 minutes.

3 Remove the pan from the heat, stir in the cheese and season with salt and pepper.

4 Spoon ^{1}/$_2$ teaspoon of the mixture on to the middle of 36 pasta squares. Brush the edges of the squares with water and top with the remaining 36 squares. Press the edges together to seal. Leave to rest for 5 minutes.

5 Bring a large pan of water to the boil, add the oil and cook the tortelloni, in batches, for 2–3 minutes. The tortelloni will rise to the surface when cooked and the pasta should be tender with a slight 'bite'. Remove from the pan with a perforated spoon and drain thoroughly.

6 Meanwhile, melt the remaining butter in a pan. Add the remaining garlic and plenty of pepper and cook for 1–2 minutes.

7 Transfer the tortelloni to serving plates and pour over the garlic butter. Garnish with grated pecorino cheese and serve immediately.

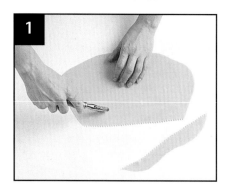

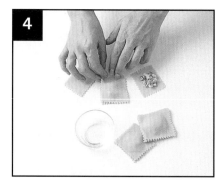

Chilli Polenta Chips

Polenta is a maize flour used in Italy in the same way as potatoes and rice. On its own it has little flavour, but combined with butter, garlic and herbs, it is completely transformed.

Serves 4

INGREDIENTS

350 g/12 oz instant polenta
2 tsp chilli powder

1 tbsp olive oil
150 ml/5 fl oz/²/₃ cup soured cream

1 tbsp chopped parsley
salt and pepper

1 Place 1.5 litres/2¾ pints/6¼ cups of water in a saucepan and bring to the boil. Add 2 teaspoons of salt and then add the polenta in a steady stream, stirring constantly.

2 Reduce the heat slightly and continue stirring for about 5 minutes. It is essential to stir the polenta, otherwise it will stick and burn. The polenta should have a thick consistency at this point and should be stiff enough to hold the spoon upright in the pan.

3 Add the chilli powder to the polenta mixture and stir well. Season to taste with a little salt and pepper.

4 Spread the polenta out on to a board or baking tray (cookie sheet) to about 4 cm/ 1½ inch thick. Leave to cool and set.

5 Cut the cooled polenta mixture into thin wedges.

6 Heat 1 tablespoon of oil in a pan. Add the polenta wedges and fry for 3–4 minutes on each side until golden and crispy. Alternatively, brush with melted butter and grill for 6–7 minutes until golden. Drain the cooked polenta on paper towels.

7 Mix the soured cream with parsley and place in a bowl.

8 Serve the polenta with the soured cream and parsley dip.

COOK'S TIP

Easy-cook instant polenta is widely available in supermarkets and is quick to make. It will keep for up to 1 week in the refrigerator. The polenta can also be baked in a preheated oven, at 200°C/400°F/ Gas Mark 6, for 20 minutes.

Polenta Kebabs (Kabobs)

Here, skewers of thyme-flavoured polenta, wrapped in Parma ham (prosciutto), are grilled or barbecued.

Serves 4

INGREDIENTS

175 g/6 oz instant polenta
175 ml/1 pint/scant 3¾ cups water
2 tbsp fresh thyme, stalks removed

8 slices Parma ham (prosciutto)
  (about 75 g/2¾ oz)
1 tbsp olive oil

salt and pepper
fresh green salad, to serve

1 Cook the polenta, using 750 ml/1 pint 7 fl oz/3¼ cups of water to 175 g/6 oz polenta, stirring occasionally. Alternatively, follow the instructions on the packet.

2 Add the fresh thyme to the polenta mixture and season to taste with salt and pepper.

3 Spread out the polenta, about 2.5 cm/1 inch thick, on to a board. Set aside to cool.

4 Using a sharp knife, cut the cooled polenta into 2.5 cm/ 1 inch cubes.

5 Cut the Parma ham (prosciutto) slices into 2 pieces lengthways. Wrap the Parma ham (prosciutto) around the polenta cubes.

6 Thread the Parma ham (prosciutto) wrapped polenta cubes on to skewers.

7 Brush the kebabs (kabobs) with a little oil and cook under a preheated grill (broiler), turning frequently, for 7–8 minutes. Alternatively, barbecue (grill) the kebabs (kabobs) until golden. Transfer to serving plates and serve with a green salad.

VARIATION

Try flavouring the polenta with chopped oregano, basil or marjoram instead of the thyme, if you prefer. You should use 3 tablespoons of chopped herbs to every 350 g/12 oz instant polenta.

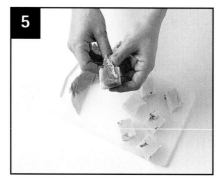

Smoked Cod Polenta

Using polenta as a crust for a gratin dish gives a lovely crispy outer texture and a smooth inside. It works well with smoked fish and chicken.

Serves 4

INGREDIENTS

350 g/12 oz instant polenta
1.5 litres/2³/₄ pints/6¹/₂ cups water
200 g/7 oz chopped frozen spinach, defrosted

50 g/1³/₄ oz/3 tbsp butter
50 g/1³/₄ oz pecorino cheese, grated
200 ml/7 fl oz/³/₄ cup milk

450 g/1 lb smoked cod fillet, skinned and boned
4 eggs, beaten
salt and pepper

1 Cook the polenta, using 1.5 litres/2¼ pints/6½ cups of water to 350 g/12 oz polenta, stirring occasionally. Alternatively, follow the instructions on the packet.

2 Stir the spinach, butter and half of the pecorino cheese into the polenta. Season to taste with salt and pepper.

3 Divide the polenta among 4 individual ovenproof dishes, spreading the polenta evenly across the bottom and up the sides of the dishes.

4 In a large frying pan (skillet), bring the milk to the boil. Add the fish and cook for 8–10 minutes, turning once, or until tender. Remove the fish with a perforated spoon.

5 Remove the pan from the heat. Pour the eggs into the milk in the pan and mix together.

6 Using a fork, flake the fish into smaller pieces and place it in the centre of the dishes.

7 Pour the milk and egg mixture over the fish.

8 Sprinkle with the remaining cheese and bake in a preheated oven at 190°C/375°F/ Gas Mark 5 for 25–30 minutes or until set and golden. Serve hot.

VARIATION

Try using 350 g/12 oz cooked chicken breast with 2 tablespoons of chopped tarragon, instead of the fish, if you prefer.

Milanese Sun-dried Tomato Risotto

A Milanese risotto can be cooked in a variety of ways – but always with saffron.
This version with sun-dried tomatoes and wine has a lovely tangy flavour.

Serves 4

INGREDIENTS

1 tbsp olive oil
25 g/1 oz/2 tbsp butter
1 large onion, finely chopped
350 g/12 oz arborio (risotto) rice,
    washed

about 15 strands saffron
150 ml/5 fl oz/^{2}/3 cup white wine
850 ml/1^1/2 pints/3^3/4 cup hot
    vegetable or chicken stock

8 sun-dried tomatoes, cut into strips
100 g/3^1/2 oz frozen peas, defrosted
50 g/1^3/4 oz Parma ham (prosciutto),
    shredded
75 g/2^3/4 oz Parmesan cheese, grated

1 Heat the oil and butter in a
large frying pan (skillet). Add
the onion and cook for 4–5
minutes or until softened.

2 Add the rice and saffron to
the frying pan (skillet),
stirring well to coat the rice in the
oil, and cook for 1 minute.

3 Add the wine and stock
slowly to the rice mixture in
the pan, a ladleful at a time,
stirring and making sure that all
the liquid is absorbed before
adding the next ladleful of liquid.

4 About half-way through
adding the stock, stir in
the tomatoes.

5 When all of the wine and
stock is incorporated, the rice
should be cooked. Test by tasting a
grain – if it is still crunchy, add a
little more water and continue
cooking. It should take at least
15 minutes to cook.

6 Stir in the peas, Parma ham
(prosciutto) and cheese. Cook
for 2–3 minutes, stirring, until hot.
Serve with extra Parmesan.

COOK'S TIP

Italian rice is a round, short-
grained variety with a nutty
flavour, which is essential for a good
risotto. Arborio is the very best kind
to use. The finished dish should
have moist but separate grains.
This is achieved by adding the hot
stock a little at a time, only adding
more when the last addition is fully
absorbed. Don't leave the risotto
to cook by itself: it needs constant
watching to see when more
liquid is required.

Wild Mushroom Risotto

This creamy risotto is flavoured with a mixture of wild and cultivated mushrooms and thyme.

Serves 4

INGREDIENTS

2 tbsp olive oil
1 large onion, finely chopped
1 garlic clove, crushed
200 g /7 oz mixed wild and cultivated
   mushrooms, such as ceps, oyster,
   porcini and button, wiped and
   sliced if large

250 g/9 oz arborio (risotto) rice,
   washed
pinch saffron threads
700 ml/1^1/$_4$ pt/scant 3 cups hot
   vegetable stock
100 g/3^1/$_2$ oz Parmesan cheese,
   grated, plus extra for serving

2 tbsp chopped thyme
salt and pepper

1 Heat the oil in a large frying pan (skillet). Add the onions and garlic and sauté for 3–4 minutes or until softened.

2 Add the mushrooms to the pan and cook for a further 3 minutes or until they are just beginning to brown.

3 Add the rice and saffron to the pan and stir to coat the rice in the oil.

4 Mix together the stock and the wine and add to the pan, a ladleful at a time. Stir the rice mixture and allow the liquid to be fully absorbed before adding more liquid, a ladleful at a time.

5 When all of the wine and stock is incorporated, the rice should be cooked. Test by tasting a grain – if it is still crunchy, add a little more water and continue cooking. It should take at least 15 minutes to cook.

6 Stir in the cheese and thyme, and season with freshly ground black pepper.

7 Transfer the risotto to serving dishes and serve sprinkled with extra Parmesan cheese.

COOK'S TIP

Wild mushrooms each have their own distinctive flavours and make a change from button mushrooms. However, they can be quite expensive, so you can always use a mixture with chestnut (crimini) or button mushrooms instead.

Genoese Seafood Risotto

The Genoese risotto is cooked in a different way from any of the other risottos. First, you cook the rice, then you prepare a sauce, then you mix the two together. The results are just as delicious though!

Serves 4

INGREDIENTS

1.2 litres/2 pints/5 cups hot fish or
    chicken stock
350 g/12 oz arborio (risotto) rice,
    washed
50 g/1³/₄ oz/3 tbsp butter

2 garlic cloves, chopped
250 g/9 oz mixed seafood, preferably
    raw, such as prawns (shrimp),
    squid, mussels, clams and (small)
    shrimps

2 tbsp chopped oregano, plus extra
    for garnishing
50 g/1³/₄ oz pecorino or Parmesan
    cheese, grated

1 In a large saucepan, bring the stock to the boil. Add the rice and cook for about 12 minutes, stirring, until the rice is tender or according to the instructions on the packet. Drain thoroughly, reserving any excess liquid.

2 Heat the butter in a large frying pan (skillet) and add the garlic, stirring.

3 Add the raw mixed seafood to the pan (skillet) and cook for 5 minutes. If the seafood is already cooked, fry for 2–3 minutes.

4 Stir the oregano into the seafood mixture in the frying pan (skillet).

5 Add the cooked rice to the pan and cook for 2–3 minutes, stirring, or until hot. Add the reserved stock if the mixture gets too sticky.

6 Add the pecorino or Parmesan cheese and mix well.

7 Transfer the risotto to warm serving dishes and serve immediately.

COOK'S TIP

The Genoese are excellent cooks, and they make particularly delicious fish dishes flavoured with the local olive oil.

Risotto-stuffed (Bell) Peppers

Sweet roasted (bell) peppers are delightful containers for a creamy risotto and especially good topped with Mozzarella cheese.

Serves 4

INGREDIENTS

4 red or orange (bell) peppers
1 tbsp olive oil
1 large onion, finely chopped
350 g/12 oz arborio (risotto) rice,
    washed
about 15 strands saffron

150 ml/¼ pint white wine
850 ml/1½ pints hot vegetable or
    chicken stock
50 g/1¾ oz/3 tbsp butter
50 g/1¾ oz pecorino cheese, grated

50 g/1¾ oz Italian sausage, such as
    felino salame or other coarse
    Italian salame, chopped
200 g/7 oz Mozzarella cheese, sliced

1 Cut the (bell) peppers in half, retaining some of the stalk. Remove the seeds.

2 Place the (bell) peppers, cut side up, under a preheated grill (broiler) for 12–15 minutes until softened and charred.

3 Meanwhile, heat the oil in a large frying pan (skillet). Add the onion and cook for 3–4 minutes or until softened. Add the rice and saffron, stirring to coat in the oil, and cook for 1 minute.

4 Add the wine and stock slowly, a ladleful at a time, making sure that all of the liquid is absorbed before adding the next ladleful of liquid. When all of the liquid is absorbed, the rice should be cooked. Test by tasting a grain – if it is still crunchy add a little more water and continue cooking. It should take at least 15 minutes to cook.

5 Stir in the butter, pecorino cheese and the chopped Italian sausage.

6 Spoon the risotto into the (bell) peppers. Top with a slice of Mozzarella and grill (broil) for 4–5 minutes or until the cheese is bubbling. Serve hot.

VARIATION

Use tomatoes instead of the (bell) peppers, if you prefer. Halve 4 large tomatoes and scoop out the seeds. Follow steps 3–6 as there is no need to roast them.

Potato Gnocchi with Tomato Sauce

Freshly made potato gnocchi are delicious, especially when they are topped with a fragrant tomato sauce.

Serves 4

INGREDIENTS

350 g/12 oz floury (mealy) potatoes (those suitable for baking or mashing), halved
75 g/2³/4 oz self-raising flour, plus extra for rolling out
2 tsp dried oregano

2 tbsp oil
1 large onion, chopped
2 garlic cloves, chopped
1 x 400g/14 oz can chopped tomatoes
¹/2 vegetable stock cube dissolved in

100ml/3¹/2 fl oz/¹/3 cup boiling water
salt and pepper
2 tbsp basil, shredded, plus whole leaves to garnish
Parmesan cheese, grated, to serve

1 Bring a large pan of water to the boil. Add the potatoes and cook for 12–15 minutes or until tender. Drain and leave to cool.

2 Peel and then mash the potatoes with the salt and pepper, sifted flour and oregano. Mix together with your hands to form a dough.

3 Heat the oil in a pan. Add the onions and garlic and cook for 3–4 minutes. Add the tomatoes and stock and cook, uncovered, for 10 minutes. Season with salt and pepper to taste.

4 Roll the potato dough into a sausage about 2.5 cm/1 inch in diameter. Cut the sausage into 2.5 cm/1 inch lengths. Flour your hands, then press a fork into each piece to create a series of ridges on one side and the indent of your index finger on the other.

5 Bring a large pan of water to the boil and cook the gnocchi, in batches, for 2–3 minutes. They should rise to the surface when cooked. Drain and keep warm.

6 Stir the basil into the tomato sauce and pour over the gnocchi. Garnish with basil leaves and freshly ground black pepper. Sprinkle with Parmesan and serve.

VARIATION

Try serving the gnocchi with Pesto Sauce (see page 110) for a change.

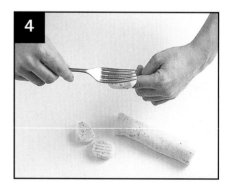

Baked Semolina Gnocchi

Semolina has a similar texture to polenta, but is slightly grainier. These gnocchi, which are delicately flavoured with cheese and thyme, are easy to make.

Serves 4

INGREDIENTS

425 ml/^{3}/$_4$ pint/1^3/$_4$ cups vegetable
  stock
100 g/3^1/$_2$ oz semolina
1 tbsp thyme, stalks removed

1 egg, beaten
50 g/1^3/$_4$ oz Parmesan cheese, grated
50 g/1^3/$_4$ oz/3 tbsp butter
2 garlic cloves, crushed

salt and pepper

1 Place the stock in a large saucepan and bring to the boil. Add the semolina in a steady trickle, stirring continuously. Keep stirring for 3–4 minutes until the mixture is thick enough to hold a spoon upright. Set aside and leave to cool slightly.

2 Add the thyme, egg and half of the cheese to the semolina mixture, and season to taste with salt and pepper.

3 Spread the semolina mixture on to a board to about 12 mm/^{1}/$_2$ inch thick. Set aside to cool and set.

4 When the semolina is cold, cut it into 2.5 cm/1 inch squares, reserving any offcuts.

5 Grease an ovenproof dish, placing the reserved offcuts in the bottom. Arrange the semolina squares on top and sprinkle with the remaining cheese.

6 Melt the butter in a pan, add the garlic and season with black pepper to taste. Pour the butter mixture over the gnocchi. Bake in a preheated oven at 220°C/425°F/Gas Mark 7 for 15–20 minutes until puffed up and golden. Serve hot.

VARIATION

Try adding ^{1}/$_2$ tablespoon of sun-dried tomato paste or 50 g/1^3/$_4$ oz finely chopped mushrooms, fried in butter, to the semolina mixture in step 2. Follow the same cooking method.

Main Dishes

*These recipes feature exciting and tempting
ways of cooking fish and meat to make a range of
satisfying meals which are typically Italian. After pasta,
fish is probably the most important source of food in
Italy. Fish markets in Italy are fascinating, with a huge
variety of fish on display, but as most fish comes from
the Mediterranean it is not always easy to find an
equivalent elsewhere. However, fresh or frozen
imported fish of all kinds is increasingly appearing
in fishmongers and supermarkets. This chapter
contains a wealth of fish and seafood recipes,
all deliciously satisfying.*

*Most meat in Italy is sold ready boned and
cut across the grain. Veal is a great favourite and
widely available. Pork is also popular, cooked with
lots of fragrant herbs, with roast pig being the
traditional dish of Umbria. Lamb is often served for
special occasions, cooked on a spit or roasted in the oven
with wine, garlic and herbs. Poultry dishes provide
some of Italy's finest food. Every part of the chicken is
used, the leftovers generally used for making soups.
Turkey, duck, goose and guinea fowl are also popular,
as is game. Wild rabbit, hare, wild boar and deer are
also available, especially in Sardinia.*

Celery & Salt Cod Casserole

Salt cod is dried and salted in order to preserve it. It has an unusual flavour, which goes particularly well with celery in this dish.

Serves 4

INGREDIENTS

250 g/9 oz salt cod, soaked overnight
1 tbsp oil
4 shallots, finely chopped
2 garlic cloves, chopped

3 celery sticks, chopped
1 x 400g/14 oz can tomatoes, chopped
150 ml/5 fl oz/²/₃ cup fish stock

50 g/1³/₄ oz pine nuts
2 tbsp roughly chopped tarragon
2 tbsp capers
crusty bread or mashed potato, to serve

1 Drain the salt cod, rinse it under plenty of running water and drain again thoroughly. Remove and discard any skin and bones. Pat the fish dry with paper towels and cut it into chunks.

2 Heat the oil in a large frying pan (skillet). Add the shallots and garlic and cook for 2–3 minutes. Add the celery and cook for a further 2 minutes, then add the tomatoes and stock.

3 Bring the mixture to the boil, reduce the heat and leave to simmer for 5 minutes.

4 Add the fish and cook for 10 minutes or until tender.

5 Meanwhile, place the pine nuts on a baking tray (cookie sheet). Place under a preheated grill (broiler) and toast for 2–3 minutes or until golden.

6 Stir the tarragon, capers and pine nuts into the fish casserole and heat gently to warm through.

7 Transfer to serving plates and serve with fresh crusty bread or mashed potato.

COOK'S TIP

Salt cod is a useful ingredient to keep in the storecupboard and once soaked, can be used in the same way as any other fish. It does, however, have a stronger flavour than normal, and it is, of course, slightly salty. It can be found in fishmongers, larger supermarkets and delicatessens.

Salt Cod Fritters

These tasty little fried cakes of mashed salt cod mixed with fennel and a little chilli make an excellent snack or main course served with vegetables and a chilli relish.

Makes 28 cakes

INGREDIENTS

100 g/3^{1}/2 oz self-raising flour
1 egg, beaten
150 ml/5 fl oz/^{2}/3 cup milk
250 g/9 oz salt cod, soaked overnight

1 small red onion, finely chopped
1 small fennel bulb, finely chopped
1 red chilli, finely chopped
2 tbsp oil

TO SERVE:
crisp salad, chilli relish, cooked rice
   and fresh vegetables

1 Sift the flour into a large bowl. Make a well in the centre of the flour and add the egg.

2 Using a wooden spoon, gradually draw in the flour, slowly adding the milk, and mix to form a smooth batter. Leave to stand for 10 minutes.

3 Drain the salt cod and rinse it under cold running water. Drain again thoroughly.

4 Remove and discard the skin and any bones from the fish, then mash the flesh with a fork.

5 Place the fish in a large bowl and combine with the onion, fennel and chilli. Add the mixture to the batter and blend together.

6 Heat the oil in a large frying pan (skillet) and, taking about 1 tablespoon of the mixture at a time, spoon it into the hot oil. Cook the fritters, in batches, for 3–4 minutes on each side until golden and slightly puffed. Keep warm while cooking the remaining mixture.

7 Serve with salad and a chilli relish for a light meal or with vegetables and rice.

COOK'S TIP

If you prefer larger fritters, use 2 tablespoons per fritter and cook for slightly longer.

Sardinian Red Mullet

*Red mullet has a beautiful pink skin, which is enhanced in this dish
by being cooked in red wine and orange juice.*

Serves 4

INGREDIENTS

50 g/1³/₄ oz sultanas
150 ml/5 fl oz/²/₃ cup red wine
2 tbsp olive oil
2 medium onions, sliced

1 courgette (zucchini) cut into
 5 cm/2 inch sticks
2 oranges
2 tsp coriander seeds, lightly crushed

4 red mullet, boned and filleted
1 x 50g/1³/₄ oz can anchovy fillets,
 drained
2 tbsp chopped, fresh oregano

1 Place the sultanas in a bowl. Pour over the red wine and leave to soak for 10 minutes.

2 Heat the oil in a large frying pan (skillet). Add the onions and sauté for 2 minutes.

3 Add the courgettes (zucchini) to the pan and fry for a further 3 minutes or until tender.

4 Using a zester, pare long, thin strips from one of the oranges. Using a sharp knife, remove the skin from both of the oranges, then segment the oranges by slicing between the lines of pith.

5 Add the orange zest to the frying pan (skillet). Add the red wine, sultanas, red mullet and anchovies to the pan and leave to simmer for 10–15 minutes or until the fish is cooked through.

6 Stir in the oregano, set aside and leave to cool. Place the mixture in a large bowl and leave to chill, covered, in the refrigerator for at least 2 hours to allow the flavours to mingle. Transfer to serving plates and serve.

COOK'S TIP

Red mullet is usually available all year round – frozen, if not fresh – from your fishmonger or supermarket. If you cannot get hold of it try using telapia. This dish can also be served warm, if you prefer.

Herrings with Hot Pesto Sauce

By making a simple pesto sauce, but omitting the cheese, it is possible to heat the paste without it becoming stringy, so it can be used as a hot sauce.

Serves 4

INGREDIENTS

4 whole herrings or small mackerel, cleaned and gutted
2 tbsp olive oil

225 g/8 oz tomatoes, peeled, deseeded and chopped
8 canned anchovy fillets, chopped

about 30 fresh basil leaves
50 g/1³/4 oz pine nuts
2 garlic cloves, crushed

1 Cook the herrings under a preheated grill (broiler) for about 8-10 minutes on each side, or until the skin is slightly charred on both sides.

2 Meanwhile, heat 1 tablespoon of the olive oil in a large saucepan.

3 Add the tomatoes and anchovies to the saucepan and cook over a medium heat for 5 minutes.

4 Meanwhile, place the basil, pine nuts, garlic and

remaining oil into a food processor and blend to form a smooth paste. Alternatively, pound the ingredients by hand in a mortar and pestle.

5 Add the pesto mixture to the saucepan containing the tomato and anchovy mixture, and stir to heat through.

6 Spoon some of the pesto sauce on to warm individual serving plates. Place the fish on top and pour the rest of the pesto sauce over the fish. Serve immediately.

COOK'S TIP

Try barbecuing (grilling) the fish for an extra char-grilled flavour, if you prefer.

Grilled (Broiled) Stuffed Sole

*A delicious stuffing of sun-dried tomatoes and fresh lemon
thyme are used to stuff whole sole.*

Serves 4

INGREDIENTS

1 tbsp olive oil
25 g/1 oz/2 tbsp butter
1 small onion, finely chopped
1 garlic clove, chopped
3 sun-dried tomatoes, chopped

2 tbsp lemon thyme
50 g/1 ¾ oz breadcrumbs
1 tbsp lemon juice
4 small whole sole, gutted and
    cleaned

salt and pepper
lemon wedges, to garnish
fresh green salad leaves, to serve

---

1 Heat the oil and butter in a frying pan (skillet) until it just begins to froth.

2 Add the onion and garlic to the frying pan (skillet) and cook, stirring, for 5 minutes until just softened.

3 To make the stuffing, mix the tomatoes, thyme, breadcrumbs and lemon juice in a bowl, and season to taste.

4 Add the stuffing mixture to the pan, and stir to mix.

5 Using a sharp knife, pare the skin from the bone inside the gut hole of the fish to make a pocket. Spoon the tomato and herb stuffing into the pocket.

6 Cook the fish, under a preheated grill (broiler), for 6 minutes on each side or until golden brown.

7 Transfer the stuffed fish to serving plates and garnish with lemon wedges. Serve immediately with fresh green salad leaves.

COOK'S TIP

*Lemon thyme (*Thymus x citriodorus*) has a delicate lemon scent and flavour. Ordinary thyme can be used instead, but mix it with 1 teaspoon of lemon rind to add extra flavour.*

Sole Fillets in Marsala & Cream

A rich wine and cream sauce makes this an excellent dinner party dish. You can make the stock the day before so it takes only minutes to cook and serve the fish.

Serves 4

INGREDIENTS

STOCK:
600 ml/1 pint/2^{1}/$_{2}$ cups water
bones and skin from the sole fillets
1 onion, peeled and halved
1 carrot, peeled and halved
3 fresh bay leaves

SAUCE;
1 tbsp olive oil
15 g/^{1}/$_{2}$ oz/1 tbsp butter
4 shallots, finely chopped
100 g/ 3^{1}/$_{2}$ oz baby button
  mushrooms, wiped and halved

1 tbsp peppercorns, lightly crushed
8 sole fillets
100 ml/3^{1}/$_{2}$ fl oz/^{1}/$_{3}$ cup Marsala
150 ml/5 fl oz/^{2}/$_{3}$ pint double (heavy)
  cream

1 To make the stock, place the water, fish bones and skin, onion, carrot and bay leaves in a saucepan and bring to the boil.

2 Reduce the heat and leave the mixture to simmer for 1 hour or until the stock has reduced to about 150 ml/5 fl oz/^{2}/$_{3}$ cup. Drain the stock through a fine sieve, discarding the bones and vegetables, and set aside.

3 To make the sauce, heat the oil and butter in a frying pan (skillet). Add the shallots and cook, stirring, for 2–3 minutes or until just softened.

4 Add the mushrooms to the frying pan (skillet) and cook, stirring, for a further 2–3 minutes or until they are just beginning to brown.

5 Add the peppercorns and sole fillets to the frying pan (skillet). Fry the sole fillets for 3–4 minutes on each side or until golden brown.

6 Pour the wine and stock over the fish and leave to simmer for 3 minutes. Remove the fish with a fish slice or a perforated spoon, set aside and keep warm.

7 Increase the heat and boil the mixture in the pan for about 5 minutes or until the sauce has reduced and thickened.

8 Pour in the cream, return the fish to the pan and heat through. Serve with the cooked vegetables of your choice.

Fresh Baked Sardines

Here, fresh sardines are baked with eggs, herbs and vegetables to form a dish similar to an omelette.

Serves 4

INGREDIENTS

2 tbsp olive oil
2 large onions, sliced into rings
3 garlic cloves, chopped
2 large courgettes (zucchini), cut into
   sticks

3 tbsp fresh thyme, stalks removed
8 sardine fillets or about 1 kg/
   2 lb 4 oz whole sardines, filleted
75 g/2³⁄₄ oz Parmesan cheese, grated

4 eggs, beaten
150 ml/5 fl oz/²⁄₃ pint milk
salt and pepper

1 Heat 1 tablespoon of the oil in a frying pan (skillet). Add the onions and garlic and sauté for 2–3 minutes.

2 Add the courgettes (zucchini) to the frying pan (skillet) and cook for about 5 minutes or until golden.

3 Stir 2 tablespoons of the thyme into the mixture.

4 Place half of the onions and courgettes (zucchini) in the base of a large ovenproof dish. Top with the sardine fillets and half of the Parmesan cheese.

5 Place the remaining onions and courgettes (zucchini) on top and sprinkle with the remaining thyme.

6 Mix the eggs and milk together in a bowl and season to taste with salt and pepper. Pour the mixture over the vegetables and sardines in the dish. Sprinkle the remaining Parmesan cheese over the top.

7 Bake in a preheated oven at 180°C/350°F/Gas Mark 4 for 20–25 minutes or until golden and set. Serve hot, straight from the oven.

VARIATION

If you cannot find sardines that are large enough to fillet, use small mackerel instead.

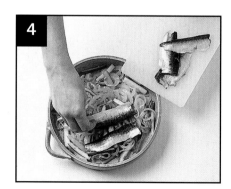

Marinated Fish

Marinating fish, for even a short period, adds a subtle flavour to the flesh and makes even simply grilled (broiled) or fried fish a delicious dish.

Serves 4

INGREDIENTS

4 whole mackerel, cleaned and
  gutted
4 tbsp chopped marjoram

2 tbsp extra virgin olive oil
finely grated rind and juice of 1 lime

2 garlic cloves, crushed
salt and pepper

1 Under gently running water, scrape the mackerel with the blunt side of a knife to remove any scales.

2 Using a sharp knife, make a slit in the stomach of the fish and cut horizontally along until the knife will go no further very easily. Gut the fish and rinse under water. You may prefer to remove the heads before cooking, but it is not necessary.

3 Using a sharp knife, cut 4–5 diagonal slashes on each side of the fish. Place the fish in a shallow, non-metallic dish.

4 To make the marinade, mix together the marjoram, olive oil, lime rind and juice, garlic and salt and pepper in a bowl.

5 Pour the mixture over the fish. Leave to marinate in the refrigerator for 30 minutes.

6 Cook the mackerel, under a preheated grill (broiler), for 5–6 minutes on each side, brushing occasionally with the reserved marinade, until golden.

7 Transfer the fish to serving plates. Pour over any remaining marinade before serving.

COOK'S TIP

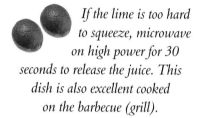

If the lime is too hard to squeeze, microwave on high power for 30 seconds to release the juice. This dish is also excellent cooked on the barbecue (grill).

Orange Mackerel

*Mackerel can be quite rich, but when it is stuffed with
oranges and toasted ground almonds it is tangy and light.*

Serves 4

INGREDIENTS

2 tbsp oil
4 spring onions (scallions), chopped
2 oranges
50 g/1³/₄ oz ground almonds

1 tbsp oats
50 g/1³/₄ oz mixed green and black
  olives, pitted and chopped

8 mackerel fillets
salt and pepper
crisp salad, to serve

1 Heat the oil in a frying pan
(skillet). Add the spring
onions (scallions) and cook for
2 minutes.

2 Finely grate the rind of the
oranges, then, using a sharp
knife, cut away the remaining skin
and white pith.

3 Using a sharp knife, segment
the oranges by cutting down
either side of the lines of pith to
loosen each segment. Do this over
a plate so that you can reserve any
juices. Cut each orange segment
in half.

4 Lightly toast the almonds,
under a preheated grill
(broiler), for 2–3 minutes or until
golden; watch them carefully as
they brown very quickly.

5 Mix the spring onions
(scallions), oranges, ground
almonds, oats and olives together
in a bowl and season to taste with
salt and pepper.

6 Spoon the orange mixture
along the centre of each fillet.
Roll up each fillet, securing it in
place with a cocktail stick
(toothpick) or skewer.

7 Bake in a preheated oven at
190°C/375°F/Gas Mark 5 for
25 minutes until the fish is tender.

8 Transfer to serving plates and
serve warm with a salad.

Italian Cod

Cod roasted with herbs and topped with a lemon and rosemary crust is a delicious main course.

Serves 4

INGREDIENTS

25 g/1 oz/2 tbsp butter
50 g/1³/₄ oz wholemeal breadcrumbs
25 g/1 oz chopped walnuts
grated rind and juice of 2 lemons

2 sprigs rosemary, stalks removed
2 tbsp chopped parsley
4 cod fillets, each about 150 g/
5¹/₂ oz

1 garlic clove, crushed
3 tbsp walnut oil
1 small red chilli, diced
salad leaves, to serve

1 Melt the butter in a large frying pan (skillet).

2 Remove the frying pan (skillet) from the heat and add the breadcrumbs, walnuts, the rind and juice of 1 lemon, half of the rosemary and half of the parsley.

3 Press the breadcrumb mixture over the top of the cod fillets. Place the cod fillets in a shallow, foil-lined roasting tin (pan).

4 Bake in a preheated oven at 200°C/400°F/Gas Mark 6 for 25–30 minutes.

5 Mix the garlic, the remaining lemon rind and juice, rosemary, parsley and chilli in a bowl. Beat in the walnut oil and mix to combine. Drizzle the dressing over the cod steaks as soon as they are cooked.

6 Transfer to serving plates and serve immediately.

VARIATION

If preferred, the walnuts may be omitted from the crust. In addition, extra virgin olive oil can be used instead of walnut oil, if you prefer.

COOK'S TIP

The 'hotness' of chillies varies so use them with caution. As a general guide, the smaller the chilli the hotter it will be.

Mussel Casserole

Mussels are not difficult to cook, just a little messy to eat. The flavours are worth it, however, and serving this dish with a finger bowl helps to keep things clean!

Serves 4

INGREDIENTS

1 kg/2 lb 4 oz mussels
150 ml/5 fl oz/²/₃ cup white wine
1 tbsp oil

1 onion, finely chopped
3 garlic cloves, chopped
1 red chilli, finely chopped

100 g/3¹/₂ oz passata (tomato paste)
1 tbsp chopped marjoram
toast or crusty bread, to serve

1 Scrub the mussels to remove any mud or sand.

2 Remove the beards from the mussels by pulling away the hairy bit between the two shells. Rinse the mussels in a bowl of clean water. Discard any mussels that do not close when they are tapped – they are dead and should not be eaten.

3 Place the mussels in a large saucepan. Pour in the wine and cook for 5 minutes, shaking the pan occasionally until the shells open. Remove and discard any mussels that do not open.

4 Remove the mussels from the saucepan with a perforated spoon. Strain the cooking liquid through a fine sieve set over a bowl, reserving the liquid.

5 Heat the oil in a large frying pan (skillet). Add the onion, garlic and chilli and cook for 4–5 minutes or until softened.

6 Add the reserved cooking liquid to the pan and cook for 5 minutes or until reduced.

7 Stir in the passata (tomato paste), marjoram and mussels and cook until hot.

8 Transfer to serving bowls and serve with toast or plenty of crusty bread to mop up the juices.

COOK'S TIP

Finger bowls are individual bowls of warm water with a slice of lemon floating in them. They are used to clean your fingers at the end of a meal.

Stuffed Squid

Whole squid are stuffed with a mixture of fresh herbs and sun-dried tomatoes and then cooked in a wine sauce.

Serves 4

INGREDIENTS

8 squid, cleaned and gutted but left whole (ask your fishmonger to do this)
6 canned anchovies, chopped
2 garlic cloves, chopped

2 tbsp rosemary, stalks removed and leaves chopped
2 sun-dried tomatoes, chopped
150 g/5^1/2 oz breadcrumbs
1 tbsp olive oil

1 onion, finely chopped
200 ml/7 fl oz/^{3}/4 cup white wine
200 ml/7 fl oz/^{3}/4 cup fish stock
cooked rice, to serve

1 Remove the tentacles from the body of the squid and chop the flesh finely.

2 Grind the anchovies, garlic, rosemary and tomatoes to a paste in a mortar and pestle.

3 Add the breadcrumbs and the chopped squid tentacles and mix. If the mixture is too dry to form a thick paste at this point, add 1 teaspoon of water.

4 Spoon the paste into the body sacs of the squid then tie a length of cotton around the end of each sac to fasten them. Do not overfill the sacs, because they will expand during cooking.

5 Heat the oil in a frying pan (skillet). Add the onion and cook, stirring, for 3–4 minutes or until golden.

6 Add the stuffed squid to the pan and cook for 3–4 minutes or until brown all over.

7 Add the wine and stock and bring to the boil. Reduce the heat, cover and then leave to simmer for 15 minutes.

8 Remove the lid and cook for a further 5 minutes until the squid is tender and the juices reduced. Serve with cooked rice.

COOK'S TIP

If you cannot buy whole squid, use squid pieces and stir the paste into the sauce with the wine and stock.

Rich Beef Stew

This slow-cooked beef stew is flavoured with oranges, red wine and porcini mushrooms.

Serves 4

INGREDIENTS

1 tbsp oil
15 g/^{1}/$_2$ oz/1 tbsp butter
225 g/8 oz baby onions, peeled and
  halved

600 g/1 lb 5 oz stewing steak, diced
  into 4 cm/1^1/$_2$ inch chunks
300 ml/^{1}/$_2$ pint/1^1/$_4$ cup beef stock
150 ml/5 fl oz/^{2}/$_3$ cup red wine
4 tbsp chopped oregano
1 tbsp sugar

1 orange
25 g/1 oz porcini or other dried
  mushrooms
225 g/8 oz fresh plum tomatoes
cooked rice or potatoes, to serve

1 Heat the oil and butter in a large frying pan (skillet). Add the onions and sauté for 5 minutes or until golden. Remove with a perforated spoon, set aside and keep warm.

2 Add the beef to the pan and cook, stirring, for 5 minutes or until browned all over.

3 Return the onions to the frying pan (skillet) and add the stock, wine, oregano and sugar, stirring to mix well. Transfer the mixture to an ovenproof casserole dish.

4 Pare the rind from the orange and cut it into strips. Slice the orange flesh into rings. Add the orange rings and the rind to the casserole. Cook in a preheated oven, at 180°C/350°F/Gas Mark 4, for 1^1/$_4$ hours.

5 Soak the porcini mushrooms for 30 minutes in a small bowl containing 4 tablespoons of warm water.

6 Peel and halve the tomatoes. Add the tomatoes, porcini mushrooms and their soaking liquid to the casserole. Cook for a further 20 minutes until the beef is tender and the juices thickened. Serve with cooked rice or potatoes.

VARIATION

Instead of fresh tomatoes, try using 8 sun-dried tomatoes, cut into wide strips, if you prefer.

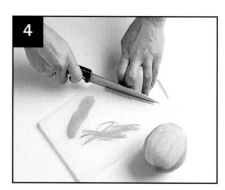

Pork with Lemon & Garlic

This is a simplified version of a traditional dish from the Marche region, on the east coast of Italy. Pork fillet pockets are stuffed with ham (prosciutto) and herbs.

Serves 4

INGREDIENTS

450 g/1 lb pork fillet
50 g/1³/₄ oz chopped almonds
2 tbsp olive oil
100 g/3¹/₂ oz raw ham (prosciutto), finely chopped

2 garlic cloves, chopped
1 tbsp fresh oregano, chopped
finely grated rind of 2 lemons
4 shallots, finely chopped

200 ml/7 fl oz/³/₄ cup ham or chicken stock
1 tsp sugar

1 Using a sharp knife, cut the pork fillet into 4 equal pieces. Place the pork between sheets of greaseproof paper and pound each piece with a meat mallet or the end of a rolling pin to flatten it.

2 Cut a horizontal slit in each piece of pork to make a pocket.

3 Place the almonds on a baking tray (cookie sheet). Lightly toast the almonds under a medium-hot grill (broiler) for 2–3 minutes or until golden.

4 Mix the almonds with 1 tablespoon of the olive oil, chopped ham (prosciutto), garlic, oregano and the finely grated rind from 1 lemon. Spoon the mixture into the pockets of the pork.

5 Heat the remaining oil in a large frying pan (skillet). Add the shallots and cook for 2 minutes.

6 Add the pork to the frying pan (skillet) and cook for 2 minutes on each side or until browned all over.

7 Add the stock to the pan, bring to the boil, cover and leave to simmer for 45 minutes or until the pork is tender. Remove the meat from the pan, set aside and keep warm.

8 Using a zester, pare the remaining lemon. Add the rind and sugar to the pan, boil for 3–4 minutes or until reduced and syrupy. Pour over the pork fillets and serve immediately.

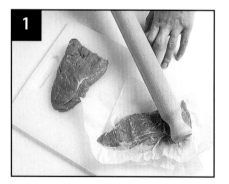

Pork Chops with Fennel & Juniper

*The addition of juniper and fennel to the pork chops gives
an unusual and delicate flavour to this dish.*

Serves 4

INGREDIENTS

¹/₂ fennel bulb
1 tbsp juniper berries, lightly crushed
about 2 tbsp olive oil

finely grated rind and juice of
1 orange

4 pork chops, each about 150 g/
5¹/₂ oz
fresh bread and a crisp salad, to serve

1 Using a sharp knife, finely chop the fennel bulb, discarding the green parts.

2 Grind the juniper berries in a mortar and pestle. Mix the crushed juniper berries with the fennel flesh, olive oil and orange rind.

3 Using a sharp knife, score a few cuts all over each chop.

4 Place the pork chops in a roasting tin (pan) or an ovenproof dish. Spoon the fennel and juniper mixture over the pork chops.

5 Carefully pour the orange juice over the top of each pork chop, cover and leave to marinate in the refrigerator for about 2 hours.

6 Cook the pork chops, under a preheated grill (broiler), for 10–15 minutes, depending on the thickness of the meat, until the meat is tender and cooked through, turning occasionally.

7 Transfer the pork chops to serving plates and serve with a crisp, fresh salad and plenty of fresh bread to mop up the cooking juices.

COOK'S TIP

Juniper berries are most commonly associated with gin, but they are often added to meat dishes in Italy for a delicate citrus flavour. They can be bought dried from most health food shops and some larger supermarkets.

Pork Cooked in Milk

This traditional dish of boned pork cooked with garlic and milk can be served hot or cold.

Serves 4

INGREDIENTS

800 g/1 lb 12 oz leg of pork, boned
1 tbsp oil
25 g/1 oz/2 tbsp butter
1 onion, chopped

2 garlic cloves, chopped
75 g/2³⁄₄ oz pancetta, diced
1.2 litres/2 pints/5 cups milk
1 tbsp green peppercorns, crushed

2 fresh bay leaves
2 tbsp marjoram
2 tbsp thyme

1 Using a sharp knife, remove the fat from the pork. Shape the meat into a neat form, tying it in place with a length of string.

2 Heat the oil and butter in a large saucepan. Add the onion, garlic and pancetta to the pan and cook for 2–3 minutes.

3 Add the pork to the pan and cook, turning occasionally, until it is browned all over.

4 Pour over the milk, add the peppercorns, bay leaves, marjoram and thyme and cook over a low heat for 1¼–1½ hours or until tender. Watch the liquid carefully for the last 15 minutes of the cooking time because it tends to reduce very quickly and will then burn. If the liquid reduces and the pork is still not tender, add another 100 ml/3½ fl oz milk and continue cooking. Reserve the cooking liquid.

5 Remove the pork from the saucepan. Using a sharp knife, cut the meat into slices. Transfer the pork slices to serving plates and serve immediately with the sauce (see Cook's Tip, right).

COOK'S TIP

As the milk reduces naturally in this dish, it forms a thick and creamy sauce, which curdles slightly but tastes delicious.

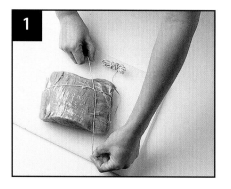

Neapolitan Pork Steaks

An Italian version of grilled pork steaks, this dish is easy to make and delicious to eat.

Serves 4

INGREDIENTS

2 tbsp olive oil
1 garlic clove, chopped
1 large onion, sliced
1 x 400 g/14 oz can tomatoes

2 tsp yeast extract
4 pork loin steaks, each about
  125 g/4^1/$_2$ oz
75 g/2 ^{3}/$_4$ oz black olives, pitted

2 tbsp fresh basil, shredded
freshly grated Parmesan cheese, to
  serve

1 Heat the oil in a large frying pan (skillet). Add the onions and garlic and cook, stirring, for 3–4 minutes or until they just begin to soften.

2 Add the tomatoes and yeast extract to the frying pan (skillet) and leave to simmer for about 5 minutes or until the sauce starts to thicken.

3 Cook the pork steaks, under a preheated grill (broiler), for 5 minutes on both sides, until the the meat is golden and cooked through. Set the pork steaks aside and keep warm.

4 Add the olives and fresh shredded basil to the sauce in the frying pan (skillet) and stir quickly to combine.

5 Transfer the steaks to warm serving plates. Top the steaks with the sauce, sprinkle with freshly grated Parmesan cheese and serve immediately.

COOK'S TIP

Parmesan is a mature and exceptionally hard cheese produced in Italy. You only need to add a little as it has a very strong flavour.

COOK'S TIP

There are many types of canned tomato available – for example plum tomatoes, or tomatoes chopped in water, or chopped sieved tomatoes (passata). The chopped variety are often canned with added flavours such as garlic, basil, onion, chilli and mixed herbs, and are a good storecupboard standby.

Roman Pan-fried Lamb

*Chunks of tender lamb, pan-fried with garlic and
stewed in red wine are a real Roman dish.*

Serves 4

INGREDIENTS

1 tbsp oil
15 g/¹/₂ oz/1 tbsp butter
600 g/1 lb 5 oz lamb (shoulder or
    leg), cut in 2.5 cm/1 inch chunks
4 garlic cloves, peeled

3 sprigs thyme, stalks removed
6 canned anchovy fillets
150 ml/5 fl oz/²/₃ cup red wine
150 ml/5 fl oz/²/₃ cup lamb or
    vegetable stock

1 tsp sugar
50 g/1³/₄ oz black olives, pitted and
    halved
2 tbsp chopped parsley, to garnish
mashed potato, to serve

1 Heat the oil and butter in a large frying pan (skillet). Add the lamb and cook for 4–5 minutes, stirring, until the meat is browned all over.

2 Using a pestle and mortar, grind together the garlic, thyme and anchovies to make a smooth paste.

3 Add the wine and lamb or vegetable stock to the frying pan (skillet). Stir in the garlic and anchovy paste together with the sugar.

4 Bring the mixture to the boil, reduce the heat, cover and leave to simmer for 30–40 minutes or until the lamb is tender. For the last 10 minutes of the cooking time, remove the lid in order to allow the sauce to reduce slightly.

5 Stir the olives into the sauce and mix to combine.

6 Transfer the lamb and the sauce to a serving bowl and garnish with freshly chopped parsley. Serve with creamy mashed potatoes.

COOK'S TIP

Rome is the capital of both the region of Lazio and Italy and thus has become a focal point for specialities from all over Italy. Food from this region tends to be fairly simple and quick to prepare, all with plenty of herbs and seasonings giving really robust flavours.

Lamb Noisettes with Bay & Lemon

*These lamb chops quickly become more elegant when the
bone is removed to make noisettes.*

Serves 4

INGREDIENTS

4 lamb chops
1 tbsp oil
15 g/^{1}/2 oz/1 tbsp butter

150 ml/5 fl oz/^{2}/3 cup white wine
150 ml/5 fl oz/^{2}/3 cup lamb or
   vegetable stock

2 bay leaves
pared rind of 1 lemon
salt and pepper

1 Using a sharp knife, carefully remove the bone from each lamb chop, keeping the meat intact. Alternatively, ask the butcher to prepare the lamb noisettes for you.

2 Shape the meat into rounds and secure with a length of string.

3 In a large frying pan (skillct), heat together the oil and butter until the mixture starts to froth. Add the lamb noisettes to the frying pan (skillet) and cook for 2–3 minutes on each side or until browned all over.

4 Remove the frying pan (skillet) fom the heat, drain off all of the fat and discard.

5 Return the frying pan (skillet) to the heat. Add the wine, stock, bay leaves and lemon rind to the frying pan (skillet) and cook for 20–25 minutes or until the lamb is tender.

6 Season the lamb noisettes and sauce to taste with a little salt and pepper.

7 Transfer to serving plates. Remove the string from each noisette and serve with the sauce.

COOK'S TIP

Your local butcher will offer you good advice on how to prepare the lamb noisettes, if you are wary of preparing them yourself.

Chicken Marengo

Napoleon's chef was ordered to cook a sumptuous meal on the eve of the battle of Marengo.
He gathered everything possible to make a feast, and this was the result.

Serves 4

INGREDIENTS

1 tbsp olive oil
8 chicken pieces
300 g/10^1/$_2$ oz passata (tomato paste)
200 ml/7 fl oz/^{3}/$_4$ cup white wine
2 tsp dried mixed herbs

8 slices white bread
40 g/1^1/$_2$ oz butter, melted
2 garlic cloves, crushed
100 g/3^1/$_2$ oz mixed mushrooms (such as button, oyster and ceps)

40 g/1^3/$_4$ oz black olives, chopped
1 tsp sugar
fresh basil, to garnish

1 Using a sharp knife, remove the bone from each of the chicken pieces.

2 Heat the oil in a large frying pan (skillet). Add the chicken pieces and cook for 4–5 minutes, turning occasionally, or until browned all over.

3 Add the passata (tomato paste), wine and mixed herbs to the frying pan (skillet). Bring to the boil and then leave to simmer for 30 minutes or until the chicken is tender and the juices run clear when a skewer is inserted into the thickest part of the meat.

4 Mix the melted butter and crushed garlic together. Lightly toast the slices of bread and brush with the garlic butter.

5 Add the remaining oil to a separate frying pan (skillet) and cook the mushrooms for 2–3 minutes or until just brown.

6 Add the olives and sugar to the chicken mixture and warm through.

7 Transfer the chicken and sauce to serving plates. Serve with the bruschetta (fried bread) and fried mushrooms.

COOK'S TIP

If you have time, marinate the chicken pieces in the wine and herbs and leave in the refrigerator for 2 hours. This will make the chicken more tender and accentuate the wine flavour of the sauce.

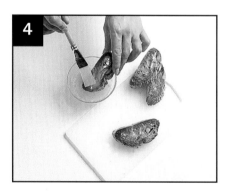

Parma-wrapped Chicken

There is a delicious surprise inside these chicken breast parcels!

Serves 4

INGREDIENTS

4 chicken breasts, skin removed
100 g/3^{1}/$_2$ oz full fat soft cheese,
flavoured with herbs and garlic

8 slices Parma ham (prosciutto)
150 ml/5 fl oz/^{2}/$_3$ cup red wine

150 ml/5 fl oz/^{2}/$_3$ cup chicken stock
1 tbsp brown sugar

1 Using a sharp knife, make a horizontal slit along the length of each chicken breast to form a pocket.

2 Beat the cheese with a wooden spoon to soften it. Spoon the cheese into the pocket of the chicken breasts.

3 Wrap 2 slices of Parma ham (prosciutto) around each chicken breast and secure in place with a length of string.

4 Pour the wine and chicken stock into a large frying pan (skillet) and bring to the boil. When the mixture is just starting to boil, add the sugar and stir to dissolve.

5 Add the chicken breasts to the mixture in the frying pan (skillet). Leave to simmer for 12–15 minutes or the chicken is tender and the juices run clear when a skewer is inserted into the thickest part of the meat.

6 Remove the chicken from the pan, set aside and keep warm.

7 Reheat the sauce and boil until reduced and thickened. Remove the string from the chicken and cut into slices. Pour the sauce over the chicken to serve.

VARIATION

Try adding 2 finely chopped sun-dried tomatoes to the soft cheese in step 2, if you prefer.

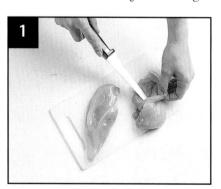

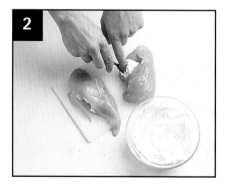

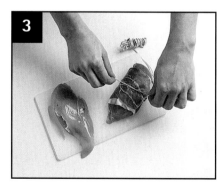

Chicken with Balsamic Vinegar

A rich caramelized sauce, flavoured with balsamic vinegar and wine,
gives this chicken dish a piquant flavour.

Serves 4

INGREDIENTS

4 chicken thighs, boned
2 garlic cloves, crushed
200 ml/7 fl oz/³/₄ cup red wine
3 tbsp white wine vinegar

1 tbsp oil
15 g/¹/₂ oz/1 tbsp butter
4 shallots
3 tbsp balsamic vinegar

2 tbsp fresh thyme
salt and pepper
cooked polenta or rice, to serve

1 Using a sharp knife, make a few slashes in the skin of the chicken. Brush the chicken with the crushed garlic and place in a non-metallic dish.

2 Pour the wine and white wine vinegar over the chicken and season to taste with salt and pepper. Cover and leave to marinate in the refrigerator overnight.

3 Remove the chicken pieces with a perforated spoon, draining well, and reserve the marinade.

4 Heat the oil and butter in a frying pan (skillet). Add the shallots and cook for 2–3 minutes or until they begin to soften.

5 Add the chicken pieces to the pan and cook for 3-4 minutes, turning, until browned all over. Reduce the heat and add half of the reserved marinade. Cover and cook for 15–20 minutes, adding more marinade when necessary.

6 Once the chicken is tender, add the balsamic vinegar and thyme and cook for a further 4 minutes.

7 Transfer the chicken and marinade to serving plates and serve with polenta or rice.

COOK'S TIP

To make the chicken pieces look a little neater, use wooden skewers to hold them together or secure them with a length of string.

Saltimbocca

The Italian name for this dish, Saltimbocca, *means 'jump into the mouth'. The stuffed rolls are quick and easy to make and taste delicious.*

Serves 4

INGREDIENTS

4 turkey fillets or 4 veal escalopes, about 450 g/1 lb in total
100 g/3³/4 oz Parma ham (prosciutto)

8 sage leaves
1 tbsp olive oil
1 onion, finely chopped

200 ml/7 fl oz/³/4 cup white wine
200 ml/7 fl oz/³/4 cup chicken stock

1 Place the turkey or veal between sheets of greaseproof paper. Pound the meat with a meat mallet or the end of a rolling pin to flatten it slightly. Cut each escalope in half.

2 Trim the Parma ham (prosciutto) to fit each piece of turkey or veal and place over the meat. Lay a sage leaf on top. Roll up the escalopes and secure with a cocktail stick (toothpick).

3 Heat the oil in a frying pan (skillet) and cook the onion for 3–4 minutes. Add the turkey or veal rolls to the pan and cook for 5 minutes until brown all over.

4 Pour the wine and stock into the pan and leave to simmer for 15 minutes if using turkey, and 20 minutes for veal, or until tender. Serve immediately.

VARIATION

Try a similar recipe called Bocconcini, *meaning 'little mouthfuls'. Follow the same method as here, but replace the sage leaf with a piece of Gruyère cheese.*

COOK'S TIP

If using turkey rather than veal, watch it carefully as turkey tends to turn dry very quickly if overcooked.

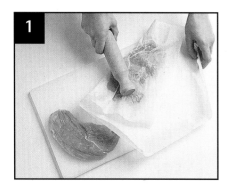

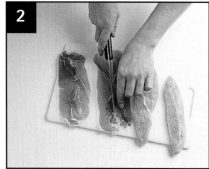

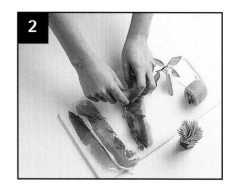

Escalopes with Italian Sausage & Capers

Anchovies are often used to enhance flavour, particularly in meat dishes.
Either veal or turkey escalopes can be used for this pan-fried dish.

Serves 4

INGREDIENTS

1 tbsp olive oil
6 canned anchovy fillets, drained
1 tbsp capers, drained
1 tbsp fresh rosemary, stalks removed

finely grated rind and juice of 1
   orange
75 g/2 $^3/_4$ oz Italian sausage, diced
3 tomatoes, skinned and chopped

4 turkey or veal escalopes, each
   about 125 g/4$^1/_2$ oz
salt and pepper
crusty bread or cooked polenta,
   to serve

1 Heat the oil in a large frying pan (skillet). Add the anchovies, capers, fresh rosemary, orange rind and juice, Italian sausage and tomatoes to the pan and cook for 5–6 minutes, stirring occasionally.

2 Meanwhile, place the turkey or veal escalopes between sheets of greasproof paper. Pound the meat with a meat mallet or the end of a rolling pin to flatten it.

3 Add the meat to the mixture in the frying pan (skillet).

Season to taste with salt and pepper, cover and cook for 3–5 minutes on each side, slightly longer if the meat is thicker.

4 Transfer to serving plates and serve with fresh crusty bread or cooked polenta.

VARIATION

Try using 4-minute steaks, slightly flattened, instead of the turkey or veal. Cook them for 4–5 minutes on top of the sauce in the pan.

COOK'S TIP

Polenta is typical of northern Italian cuisine. It is often fried or toasted and used to mop up the juices of the main course.

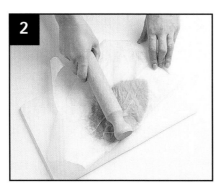

Italian Sausage & Bean Casserole

*In this traditional Tuscan dish, Italian sausages are cooked
with cannelini beans and tomatoes.*

Serves 4

INGREDIENTS

8 Italian sausages
1 tbsp olive oil
1 large onion, chopped
2 garlic cloves, chopped

1 green (bell) pepper
225g/8oz fresh tomatoes, skinned
and chopped or 1 x 400 g/14 oz
can tomatoes, chopped

2 tbsp sun-dried tomato paste
1 x 400g/14 oz can cannelini beans
mashed potato or rice, to serve

1 Deseed the (bell) pepper and cut it into thin strips.

2 Prick the Italian sausages all over with a fork. Cook them, under a preheated grill (broiler), for 10–12 minutes, turning occasionally, until brown all over. Set aside and keep warm.

3 Heat the oil in a large frying pan (skillet). Add the onion, garlic and (bell) pepper to the frying pan (skillet) and cook for 5 minutes, stirring occasionally, or until softened.

4 Add the tomatoes to the frying pan (skillet) and leave the mixture to simmer for about 5 minutes, stirring occasionally, or until slightly reduced and thickened.

5 Stir the sun-dried tomato paste, cannelini beans and Italian sausages into the mixture in the frying pan (skillet). Cook for 4–5 minutes or until the mixture is piping hot. Add 4–5 tablespoons of water, if the mixture becomes too dry during cooking.

6 Transfer the Italian sausage and bean casserole to serving plates and serve with mashed potato or cooked rice.

COOK'S TIP

Italian sausages are coarse in texture and have quite a strong flavour. They can be found in specialist sausage shops, Italian delicatessens and some larger supermarkets. They are replaceable in this recipe only by game sausages.

Pizzas & Breads

There is little to beat the irresistible aroma and taste of a freshly made pizza cooked in a wood-fired brick oven. However, a homemade dough base and a freshly made tomato sauce will give you the closest thing possible to an authentic Italian pizza. Pizzas can have every imaginable type of topping. There are endless varieties of salamis and cured meats, hams and sausages which all make excellent toppings. Canned or fresh fish or seafood are also good. Vegetables of all kinds make the most tempting and attractive pizza toppings. Choose the best quality vegetables and herbs for maximum flavour. A variety of antipasti, *such as artichoke hearts, sun-dried tomatoes, sliced (bell) peppers and mushrooms, are sold in jars of olive oil and these make the most delicious and convenient toppings. You can also use the oil from the jar to drizzle over the pizza before baking to keep it moist.*

There is nothing quite like the smell of freshly baked bread, and the Italians do it so well. They combine the sun-drenched flavours of the Mediterranean with delicious fresh and crusty bread – a winning combination. You can use the breads in this chapter to mop up the delicious juices from a range of Italian dishes, or you can eat them on their own as a tasty snack.

Pizza Margherita

Pizza means 'pie' in Italian. The fresh bread dough is not difficult to make but it does take a little time.

Serves 4

INGREDIENTS

BASIC PIZZA DOUGH:
7 g/^{1}/$_4$ oz dried yeast
1 tsp sugar
250 ml/9 fl oz/1 cup hand-hot water
350 g/12 oz strong flour
1 tsp salt
1 tbsp olive oil

TOPPING:
1 x 400 g/14 oz can tomatoes, chopped
2 garlic cloves, crushed
2 tsp dried basil
1 tbsp olive oil
2 tbsp tomato purée

100 g/3^1/$_2$ oz Mozzarella cheese, chopped
2 tbsp freshly grated Parmesan cheese
salt and pepper

1 Place the yeast and sugar in a measuring jug and mix with 50 ml/2 fl oz/4 tbsp of the water. Leave the yeast mixture in a warm place for 15 minutes or until frothy.

2 Mix the flour with the salt and make a well in the centre. Add the oil, the yeast mixture and the remaining water. Using a wooden spoon, mix to form a dough.

3 Turn the dough out on to a floured surface and knead for 4–5 minutes or until smooth.

4 Return the dough to the bowl, cover with an oiled sheet of cling film (plastic wrap) and leave to rise for 30 minutes or until doubled in size.

5 Knead the dough for 2 minutes. Stretch the dough with your hands, then place it on an oiled baking tray (cookie sheet), pushing out the edges until even and to the shape required. The dough should be no more than 6 mm/^{1}/$_4$ inch thick because it will rise during cooking.

6 To make the topping, place the tomatoes, garlic, dried basil, olive oil and salt and pepper to taste in a large frying pan (skillet) and leave to simmer for 20 minutes or until the sauce has thickened. Stir in the tomato purée and leave to cool slightly.

7 Spread the topping evenly over the pizza base. Top with the Mozzarella and Parmesan cheeses and bake in a preheated oven at 200°C/400°F/Gas Mark 6 for 20–25 minutes. Serve hot.

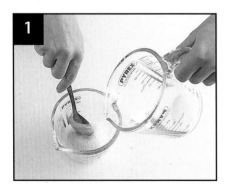

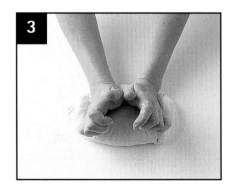

Gorgonzola Pizza

An unusual combination of blue Gorgonzola cheese and pears combine to give a colourful pizza.
The wholemeal base adds a nutty flavour and texture.

Serves 4

INGREDIENTS

PIZZA DOUGH:
7 g/^{1}/$_4$ oz dried yeast
1 tsp sugar
250 ml/9 fl oz/1 cup hand-hot water
175 g/6 oz wholemeal flour
175 g/6 oz strong white flour

1 tsp salt
1 tbsp olive oil

TOPPING:
400 g/14 oz pumpkin or squash,
  peeled and cubed

1 tbsp olive oil
1 pear, cored, peeled and sliced
100 g 3^1/$_2$ oz Gorgonzola cheese
1 sprig fresh rosemary, to garnish

1 Place the yeast and sugar in a measuring jug and mix with 50 ml/2 fl oz/4 tbsp of the water. Leave the yeast mixture in a warm place for 15 minutes or until frothy.

2 Mix both of the flours with the salt and make a well in the centre. Add the oil, the yeast mixture and the remaining water. Using a wooden spoon, mix to form a dough.

3 Turn the dough out on to a floured surface and knead for 4–5 minutes or until smooth.

4 Return the dough to the bowl, cover with an oiled sheet of cling film (plastic wrap) and leave to rise for 30 minutes or until doubled in size.

5 Remove the dough from the bowl. Knead the dough for 2 minutes. Using a rolling pin, roll out the dough to form a long oval shape, then place it on an oiled baking tray (cookie sheet), pushing out the edges until even. The dough should be no more than 6 mm/^{1}/$_4$ inch thick because it will rise during cooking.

6 To make the topping, place the pumpkin in a shallow roasting tin (pan). Drizzle with the olive oil and cook under a preheated grill (broiler) for 20 minutes or until soft and lightly golden.

7 Top the dough with the pear and the pumpkin, brushing with the oil from the tin (pan). Sprinkle over the Gorgonzola. Bake in a preheated oven, at 200°C/400°F/Gas Mark 6 for 15 minutes or until the base is golden. Garnish with a sprig of rosemary.

Onion, Ham & Cheese Pizza

This pizza was a favourite of the Romans. It is slightly unusual because the topping is made without a tomato sauce base.

Serves 4

INGREDIENTS

1 portion of Basic Pizza Dough (see page 196)

TOPPING:
2 tbsp olive oil

250 g/9 oz onions, sliced into rings
2 garlic cloves, crushed
1 red (bell) pepper, diced
100 g/3 1/2 oz raw ham (prosciutto), cut into strips

100 g/3 1/2 oz Mozzarella cheese, sliced
2 tbsp rosemary, stalks removed and roughly chopped

1 Place the yeast and sugar in a measuring jug and mix with 50 ml/2 fl oz/4 tbsp of the water. Leave the yeast mixture in a warm place for 15 minutes or until frothy.

2 Mix the flour with the salt and make a well in the centre. Add the oil, the yeast mixture and the remaining water. Using a wooden spoon, mix to form a dough.

3 Turn the dough out on to a floured surface and knead for 4–5 minutes or until smooth. Return the dough to the bowl, cover with an oiled sheet of cling

film (plastic wrap) and leave to rise for 30 minutes or until doubled in size.

4 Remove the dough from the bowl. Knead the dough for 2 minutes. Using a rolling pin, roll out the dough to form a square shape, then place it on an oiled baking tray (cookie sheet), pushing out the edges until even. The dough should be no more than 6 mm/1/4 inch thick because it will rise during cooking.

5 To make the topping, heat the oil in a pan. Add the onions

and garlic and cook for 3 minutes. Add the (bell) pepper and fry for a further 2 minutes.

6 Cover the pan and cook the vegetables over a low heat for 10 minutes, stirring occasionally, until the onions are slightly caramelized. Leave to cool slightly.

7 Spread the topping evenly over the pizza base. Place strips of ham (prosciutto), Mozzarella and rosemary over the top. Bake in a preheated oven at 200°C/400°F/Gas Mark 6 for 20–25 minutes. Serve hot.

Sun-dried Tomatoes & Ricotta Pizza

This is a traditional dish from the Calabrian Mountains in southern Italy, where it is made with naturally sun-dried tomatoes and ricotta cheese.

Serves 4

INGREDIENTS

1 portion Basic Pizza Dough (see page 196)

TOPPING:
4 tbsp sun-dried tomato paste
150g/5½ oz ricotta cheese

10 sun-dried tomatoes
1 tbsp fresh thyme
salt and pepper

1 Place the yeast and sugar in a measuring jug and mix with 50 ml/2 fl oz/4 tbsp of the water. Leave the yeast mixture in a warm place for 15 minutes or until frothy.

2 Mix the flour with the salt and make a well in the centre. Add the oil, the yeast mixture and the remaining water. Using a wooden spoon, mix to form a dough.

3 Turn the dough out on to a floured surface and knead for 4–5 minutes or until smooth.

4 Return the dough to the bowl, cover with an oiled sheet of cling film (plastic wrap)

and leave to rise for 30 minutes or until doubled in size.

5 Remove the dough from the bowl. Knead the dough for 2 minutes.

6 Using a rolling pin, roll out the dough to form a circle, then place it on an oiled baking tray (cookie sheet), pushing out the edges until even. The dough should be no more than 6 mm/¼ inch thick because it will rise during cooking.

7 Spread the sun-dried tomato paste over the dough, then add spoonfuls of ricotta.

8 Cut the sun-dried tomatoes into strips and arrange these on top of the pizza.

9 Sprinkle the thyme, and salt and pepper to taste over the top of the pizza. Bake in a preheated oven at 200°C/400°F/ Gas Mark 6 for 30 minutes or until the crust is golden. Serve hot.

COOK'S TIP

The dough for crispy-based pizzas should be rolled out as thinly as possible.

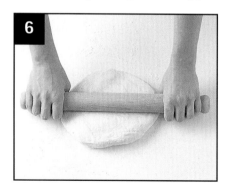

Mushroom Pizza

Juicy mushrooms and stringy Mozzarella top this tomato-based pizza.
Use wild mushrooms or a combination of wild and cultivated mushrooms.

Serves 4

INGREDIENTS

1 portion Basic Pizza Dough (see
  page 196)

TOPPING:
1 x 400g/14 oz can chopped tomatoes

2 garlic cloves, crushed
1 tsp dried basil
1 tbsp olive oil
2 tbsp tomato purée
200 g/7 oz mushrooms

150 g/5$\frac{1}{2}$ oz Mozzarella cheese,
  grated
salt and pepper
basil leaves, to garnish

1 Place the yeast and sugar in a measuring jug and mix with 50 ml/2 fl oz/4 tbsp of the water. Leave the yeast mixture in a warm place for 15 minutes or until frothy.

2 Mix the flour with the salt and make a well in the centre. Add the oil, the yeast mixture and the remaining water. Using a wooden spoon, mix to form a dough.

3 Turn the dough out on to a floured surface and knead for 4–5 minutes or until smooth. Return the dough to the bowl, cover with an oiled sheet of cling

film (plastic wrap) and leave to rise for 30 minutes or until doubled in size.

4 Remove the dough from the bowl. Knead the dough for 2 minutes. Using a rolling pin, roll out the dough to form an oval or a circular shape, then place it on an oiled baking tray (cookie sheet), pushing out the edges until even. The dough should be no more than 6 mm/$\frac{1}{4}$ inch thick because it will rise during cooking.

5 Using a sharp knife, chop the mushrooms into slices.

6 To make the topping, place the tomatoes, garlic, dried basil, olive oil and salt and pepper in a large pan and simmer for 20 minutes or until the sauce has thickened. Stir in the tomato purée and leave to cool slightly.

7 Spread the sauce over the base of the pizza, top with the sliced mushrooms and scatter over the Mozzarella.

8 Bake in a preheated oven at 200°C/400°F/Gas Mark 6 for 25 minutes. Just before serving, garnish with fresh basil leaves.

Mini-pizzas

Pizette, as they are known in Italy, are tiny pizzas. This quantity will make 8 individual pizzas, or 16 cocktail pizzas to go with drinks.

Makes 8

INGREDIENTS

1 portion Basic Pizza Dough (see page 196)

TOPPING:
2 courgettes (zucchini)
100 g/3^1/$_2$ oz passata (tomato paste)
75 g/2^3/$_4$ oz pancetta, diced

50 g/1^3/$_4$ oz black olives, pitted and chopped
1 tbsp mixed dried herbs
2 tbsp olive oil

1 Place the yeast and sugar in a measuring jug and mix with 50 ml/2 fl oz/4 tbsp of the water. Leave the yeast mixture in a warm place for 15 minutes or until frothy.

2 Mix the flour with the salt and make a well in the centre. Add the oil, the yeast mixture and the remaining water. Using a wooden spoon, mix to form a dough.

3 Turn the dough out on to a floured surface and knead for 4–5 minutes or until smooth. Return the dough to the bowl, cover with an oiled sheet of cling film (plastic wrap) and leave to rise for 30 minutes or until doubled in size.

4 Knead the dough for 2 minutes and divide it into 8 balls. Roll out each portion thinly to form circles or squares, then place them on an oiled baking tray (cookie sheet), pushing out the edges until even. The dough should be no more than 6 mm/^{1}/$_4$ inch thick because it will rise during cooking.

5 To make the topping, grate the courgettes (zucchini) finely. Cover with paper towels and leave to stand for 10 minutes to absorb some of the juices.

6 Spread 2–3 teaspoons of the passata (tomato paste) over the pizza bases and top each with the grated courgettes (zucchini), pancetta and olives. Season with freshly ground black pepper, a sprinkling of mixed dried herbs and drizzle with olive oil.

7 Bake in a preheated oven at 200°C/400°F/Gas Mark 6 for 15 minutes or until crispy. Season and serve hot.

Pizza with Tomato Sauce & Roasted (Bell) Peppers

This pizza, which is similar to the French Pissaladière, is made with a pastry base flavoured with cheese and topped with a delicious tomato sauce and roasted (bell) peppers.

Serves 4

INGREDIENTS

225 g/8 oz plain (all-purpose) flour
125 g/4^1/$_2$ oz butter, diced
^{1}/$_2$ tsp salt
2 tbsp dried Parmesan cheese
1 egg, beaten
2 tbsp cold water

2 tbsp olive oil
1 large onion, finely chopped
1 garlic clove, chopped
1 x 400 g/14 oz can chopped tomatoes
4 tbsp concentrated tomato purée

1 red (bell) pepper, halved
5 sprigs of thyme, stalks removed
6 black olives, pitted and halved
25 g/1 oz Parmesan cheese, grated

1 Sift the flour and rub in the butter to make breadcrumbs. Stir in the salt and dried Parmesan. Add the egg and 1 tablespoon of the water and mix with a round-bladed knife. Add more water if necessary to make a soft dough. Cover with cling film (plastic wrap) and chill for 30 minutes.

2 Meanwhile, heat the oil in a frying pan (skillet) and cook the onions and garlic for about 5 minutes or until golden. Add the tomatoes and cook for 8–10 minutes. Stir in the tomato purée.

3 Place the (bell) peppers, skin-side up, on a baking tray (cookie sheet) and cook under a preheated gril (broiler) for 15 minutes until charred. Place in a plastic bag and leave to sweat for 10 minutes. Peel off the skin and slice the flesh into thin strips.

4 Roll out the dough to fit a 23 cm/ 9 inch loose base fluted flan tin (pan). Line with foil and bake in a preheated oven at 200°C/400°F/Gas Mark 6 for 10 minutes or until just set. Remove the foil and bake for a further 5 minutes until lightly golden. Leave to cool slightly.

5 Spoon the tomato sauce over the pastry base and top with the (bell) peppers, thyme, olives and fresh Parmesan. Return to the oven for 15 minutes or until the pastry is crisp. Serve warm or cold.

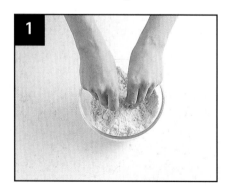

Folded-over Pizza

A calzone, as this pizza is known, can have many different fillings. Here, cured meats mix well with Mozzarella and Parmesan cheese.

Makes 4 large or 8 small calzone

INGREDIENTS

1 portion of Basic Pizza Dough (see page 196)
freshly grated Parmesan cheese, to serve

TOPPING:
75 g/2³/₄ oz mortadella or other Italian pork sausage, chopped
50 g/1³/₄ oz Italian sausage, chopped
50 g/1³/₄ oz Parmesan cheese, sliced

100 g/3¹/₂ oz Mozzarella, cut into chunks
2 tomatoes, diced
4 tbsp fresh oregano
salt and pepper

1 Place the yeast and sugar in a measuring jug and mix with 50 ml/2 fl oz/4 tbsp of the water. Leave the yeast mixture in a warm place for 15 minutes or until frothy.

2 Mix the flour with the salt and make a well in the centre. Add the oil, the yeast mixture and the remaining water. Using a wooden spoon, mix to form a dough.

3 Turn the dough out on to a floured surface and knead for 4–5 minutes or until smooth. Return the dough to the bowl, cover with an oiled sheet of cling film (plastic wrap) and leave to rise for 30 minutes or until doubled in size.

4 Knead the dough for 2 minutes and divide it into 4 pieces. Roll out each portion thinly to form circles. Place them on an oiled baking tray (cookie sheet). The dough should be no more than 6 mm/¹/₄ inch thick because it will rise during cooking.

5 To make the topping, place both Italian sausages, the Parmesan and the Mozzarella on one side of each circle. Top with the tomatoes and oregano. Season to taste with salt and pepper.

6 Brush around the edges of the dough with a little water then fold over the circle to form a pasty shape. Squeeze the edges together to seal so that none of the filling leaks out during cooking.

7 Bake in a preheated oven at 200°C/400°F/Gas Mark 6 for 10–15 minutes or until golden. If you are making the smaller pizzas, reduce the cooking time to 8–10 minutes. Serve with freshly grated Parmesan cheese.

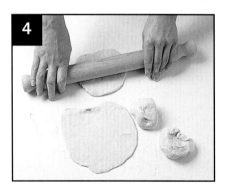

Pizza with Creamy Ham & Cheese Sauce

This is a traditional pizza which uses a pastry case and béchamel sauce to make a type of savoury flan. Grating the pastry gives it a lovely nutty texture.

Serves 4

INGREDIENTS

250 g/9 oz flaky pastry, well chilled
40 g/1¹/₂ oz/3 tbsp butter
1 red onion, chopped
1 garlic clove, chopped
40 g/1¹/₂ oz strong flour

300 ml/¹/₂ pint/1¹/₄ cups milk
50 g/1³/₄ oz Parmesan cheese, finely grated, plus extra for sprinkling
2 eggs, hard-boiled (hard-cooked), cut into quarters

100 g/3¹/₂ oz Italian pork sausage, such as feline salame, cut into strips
salt and pepper
sprigs of fresh thyme, to garnish

1 Fold the sheet of flaky pastry in half and coarsely grate it into 4 individual flan tins, 10 cm/ 4 inch across. Using a floured fork, press the pastry flakes down lightly so that they are even, there are no holes and the pastry comes up the sides of the tin.

2 Line with foil and bake blind in a preheated oven at 220°C/ 425°F/Gas Mark 7 for 10 minutes. Reduce the heat to 200°C/400°F/ Gas Mark 6, remove the foil and cook for a further 15 minutes or until golden and set.

3 Heat the butter in a pan. Add the onion and garlic and cook for 5–6 minutes or until softened.

4 Add the flour, stirring well to coat the onions. Gradually stir in the milk to make a thick sauce. Season well with salt and pepper and then stir in the Parmesan cheese. Do not reheat once the cheese has been added or the sauce will become stringy.

5 Spread the sauce over the pastry cases. Decorate with the egg and strips of sausage.

6 Sprinkle with a little extra Parmesan cheese, return to the oven and bake for 5 minutes, just to heat through.

7 Serve immediately, garnished with sprigs of fresh thyme.

COOK'S TIP

This pizza is just as good cold, but do not prepare it too far in advance as the pastry will become soggy.

Olive Oil Bread with Cheese

This flat cheese bread is sometimes called foccacia. *It is delicious served with* antipasto *or simply on its own.*

Makes 1 loaf

INGREDIENTS

15 g/¹/₂ oz dried yeast
1 tsp sugar
250 ml/9 fl oz hand-hot water

350 g/12 oz strong flour
1 tsp salt
3 tbsp olive oil

200 g/7 oz pecorino cheese, cubed
¹/₂ tbsp fennel seeds, lightly crushed

1 Mix the yeast with the sugar and 100 ml/3¹/₂ fl oz/8 tbsp of the water. Leave to ferment in a warm place for about 15 minutes.

2 Mix the flour with the salt. Add 1 tbsp of the oil, the yeast mixture and the remaining water to form a smooth dough. Knead the dough for 4 minutes.

3 Divide the dough into 2 equal portions. Roll out each portion to a form a round 6 mm/¹/₄ inch thick. Place 1 round on a baking tray (cookie sheet). Scatter the cheese and half of the fennel seeds evenly over the round.

4 Place the second round on top and squeeze the edges together to seal so that the filling does not leak during cooking.

5 Using a sharp knife, make a few slashes in the top of the dough and brush with the remaining olive oil.

6 Sprinkle with the remaining fennel seeds and leave to rise for 20–30 minutes.

7 Bake in a preheated oven at 200°C/400°F/Gas Mark 6 for 30 minutes or until golden. Serve immediately.

COOK'S TIP

Pecorino is a hard, quite salty cheese, which is sold in most large supermarkets and Italian delicatessens. If you cannot obtain pecorino, use strong Cheddar or Parmesan cheese instead.

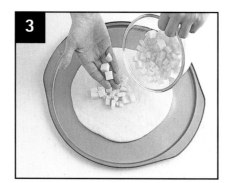

Roman Focaccia

Roman focaccia *makes a delicious snack on its own or serve it with cured meats and salad for a quick supper.*

Makes 16 squares

INGREDIENTS

7 g/¹/₄ oz dried yeast
1 tsp sugar
300 ml/¹/₂ pint/1¹/₄ cups hand-hot
  water

450 g/1 lb strong white flour
2 tsp salt
3 tbsp rosemary, chopped
2 tbsp olive oil

450 g/1 lb mixed red and white
  onions, sliced into rings
4 garlic cloves, sliced

1 Place the yeast and the sugar in a small bowl and mix with 100 ml/3¹/₂ fl oz/8 tablespoons of the water. Leave to ferment in a warm place for 15 minutes.

2 Mix the flour with the salt in a large bowl. Add the yeast mixture, half of the rosemary and the remaining water and mix to form a smooth dough. Knead the dough for 4 minutes.

3 Cover the dough with oiled cling film (plastic wrap) and leave to rise for 30 minutes or until doubled in size.

4 Meanwhile, heat the oil in a large pan. Add the onions and garlic and fry for 5 minutes or until softened. Cover the pan and continue to cook for a further 7–8 minutes or until the onions are lightly caramelized.

5 Remove the dough from the bowl and knead it again for 1–2 minutes.

6 Roll the dough out to form a square shape. The dough should be no more than 6 mm/¹/₄ inch thick because it will rise during cooking. Place the dough

on to a large baking tray (cookie sheet), pushing out the edges until even.

7 Spread the onions over the dough, and sprinkle with the remaining rosemary.

8 Bake in a preheated oven 200°C/400°F/Gas Mark 6 for 25–30 minutes or until golden. Cut into 16 squares and serve immediately.

Sun-dried Tomato Loaf

This delicious tomato bread is great with cheese or soup or to make an unusual sandwich.

makes 1 loaf

INGREDIENTS

7 g/¹/₄ oz dried yeast
1 tsp sugar
300 ml/1¹/₄ cups hand-hot water

1 tsp salt
2 tsp dried basil
450 g/1 lb strong white flour

2 tbsp sun-dried tomato paste or tomato purée
12 sun-dried tomatoes, cut into strips

1 Place the yeast and sugar in a bowl and mix with 100 ml/ 3½ fl oz/8 tablespoons of the water. Leave to ferment in a warm place for 15 minutes.

2 Place the flour in a bowl and stir in the salt. Make a well in the dry ingredients and add the basil, the yeast mixture, tomato paste and half of the remaining water. Using a wooden spoon, draw the flour into the liquid and mix to form a dough, adding the rest of the water gradually.

3 Turn out the dough on to a floured surface and knead for

5 minutes or until smooth. Cover with oiled cling film (plastic wrap) and leave in a warm place to rise for about 30 minutes or until doubled in size.

4 Lightly grease a 900 g/2 lb loaf tin (pan).

5 Remove the dough from the bowl and knead in the sun-dried tomatoes. Knead again for 2–3 minutes.

6 Place the dough in the tin (pan) and leave to rise for 30–40 minutes. Once it has doubled in size again, bake in a

preheated oven at 190°C/375°F/ Gas Mark 5 for 30–35 minutes or until golden and the base sounds hollow when tapped.

COOK'S TIP

You could make mini sun-dried tomato loaves for children. Divide the dough into 8 equal portions, leave to rise and bake in mini-loaf tins (pans) for 20 minutes. Alternatively, make 12 small rounds, leave to rise and bake as rolls for 12–15 minutes.

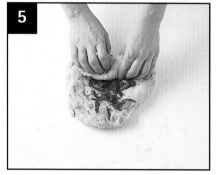

Roasted (Bell) Pepper Bread

(Bell) peppers become sweet and mild when they are roasted and make this bread delicious.

Serves 4

INGREDIENTS

1 red (bell)pepper, halved and deseeded
1 yellow (bell) pepper, halved and deseeded

2 sprigs rosemary
1 tbsp olive oil
7 g/^{1}/$_4$ oz dried yeast
1 tsp sugar

300 ml/^{1}/$_2$ pint/1^1/$_4$ cups hand-hot water
450 g/1 lb strong white flour
1 tsp salt

1 Grease a 23 cm/9 inch deep round cake tin (pan).

2 Place the (bell) peppers and rosemary in a shallow roasting tin (pan). Pour over the oil and roast in a preheated oven, at 200°C/400°F/Gas Mark 6, for 20 minutes or until slightly charred. Remove the skin from the (bell) peppers and cut the flesh into slices.

3 Place the yeast and sugar in a small bowl and mix with 100 ml/3^1/$_2$ fl oz/8 tablespoons of hand-hot water. Leave to ferment in a warm place for about 15 minutes.

4 Mix the flour and salt together in a large bowl.Stir in the yeast mixture and the remaining water and mix to form a smooth dough.

5 Knead the dough for about 5 minutes until smooth. Cover with oiled cling film (plastic wrap) and leave to rise for about 30 minutes or until doubled in size.

6 Cut the dough into 3 equal portions. Roll the portions into rounds slightly larger than the cake tin (pan).

7 Place 1 round in the base of the tin (pan) so that it reaches

up the sides of the tin (pan) by about 2 cm/^{3}/$_4$ inch. Top with half of the (bell) pepper mixture.

8 Place the second round of dough on top, followed by the remaining (bell) pepper mixture. Place the last round of dough on top, pushing the edges of the dough down the sides of the tin (pan).

9 Cover the dough with oiled cling film (plastic wrap) and leave to rise for 30–40 minutes. Place in the preheated oven and bake for 45 minutes until golden or the base sounds hollow when lightly tapped. Serve warm.

Green Easter Pie

This traditional Easter risotto pie is from Piedmont in northern Italy.
Serve it warm or chilled in slices.

Serves 4

INGREDIENTS

2 tbsp olive oil
1 onion, chopped
2 garlic cloves, chopped
200 g/7 oz arborio (risotto) rice
700 ml/1¼ pint/scant 3 cups hot
   chicken or vegetable stock

125 ml/4 fl oz/scant ½ cup white
   wine
50 g/1¾ oz Parmesan cheese, grated
100 g/3½ oz frozen peas, defrosted
80 g/3 oz rocket (arugula)
2 tomatoes, diced

4 eggs, beaten
3 tbsp fresh marjoram, chopped
50 g/1¾ oz breadcrumbs
salt and pepper

1 Light grease and then line the base of a 23 cm/9 inch deep cake tin (pan).

2 Using a sharp knife, roughly chop the rocket (arugula).

3 Heat the oil in a large frying pan (skillet). Add the onion and garlic and cook for 4–5 minutes or until softened.

4 Add the rice to the mixture in the frying pan (skillet), mix well to combine, then begin adding the stock a ladleful at a time. Wait until all of the stock has been absorbed before adding another ladleful of liquid.

5 Continue to cook the mixture, adding the wine, until the rice is tender. This will take at least 15 minutes.

6 Stir in the Parmesan cheese, peas, rocket (arugula), tomatoes, eggs and 2 tablespoons of the marjoram. Season to taste with salt and pepper.

7 Spoon the risotto into the tin (pan) and level the surface by pressing down with the back of a wooden spoon.

8 Top with the breadcrumbs and the remaining marjoram.

9 Bake in a preheated oven, at 180°C/350°F/Gas Mark 4, for 30 minutes or until set. Cut into slices and serve immediately.

Spinach & Ricotta Pie

*This puff pastry pie looks impressive and is actually
very easy to make. Serve it hot or cold.*

Serves 4

INGREDIENTS

225 g/8 oz spinach
25 g/1 oz pine nuts
100 g/3¹/₂ oz ricotta cheese

2 large eggs, beaten
50 g/1³/₄ oz ground almonds
40 g/1¹/₂ oz Parmesan cheese, grated

250 g/9 oz puff pastry, defrosted if
 frozen
1 small egg, beaten

1 Rinse the spinach, place in a large saucepan and cook for 4-5 minutes until wilted. Drain thoroughly. When the spinach is cool enough to handle, squeeze out the excess liquid.

2 Place the pine nuts on a baking tray (cookie sheet) and lightly toast under a preheated grill (broiler) for 2–3 minutes or until golden.

3 Place the ricotta, spinach and eggs in a bowl and mix together. Add the pine nuts, beat well, then stir in the ground almonds and Parmesan cheese.

4 Roll out the puff pastry and make 2 x 20 cm/8 inch squares. Trim the edges, reserving the pastry trimmings.

5 Place 1 pastry square on a baking tray (cookie sheet). Spoon over the spinach mixture, keeping within 12 mm/¹/₂ inch of the edge of the pastry. Brush the edges with beaten egg and place the second square over the top.

6 Using a round-bladed knife, press the pastry edges together by tapping along the sealed edge. Use the pastry trimmings to make leaves to decorate the pie.

7 Brush the pie with the beaten egg and bake in a preheated oven, at 220°C/425°F/Gas Mark 8, for 10 minutes. Reduce the oven temperature to 190°C/375°F/ Gas Mark 5 and bake for a further 25–30 minutes. Serve hot.

COOK'S TIP

Spinach is very nutritious as it is full of iron – this is particularly important for women and elderly people who may lack this in their diet.

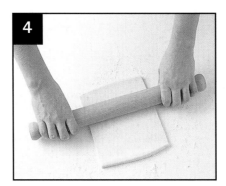

Desserts

The Italians love their desserts, but when there is a special gathering or celebration, then a special effort is made and the delicacies appear. The Sicilians are said to have the sweetest tooth of all, and many Italian desserts are thought to have originated there. You have to go a very long way to beat a Sicilian ice cream – they truly are the best in the world!

Fresh fruit also features in many Italian desserts – oranges are often peeled and served whole, marinated in a fragrant syrup and liqueur. For a deliciously fruity dessert, try Sicilian Orange & Almond Cake, Orange & Grapefruit Salad or the intoxicating flavour of Marinated Peaches.

Chocolate, too, is popular in Italy – sample Rich Chocolate Loaf and the all-time favourite Tiramisu for a deliciously wicked end to a meal. Whatever your preference, there is sure to be an Italian dessert to tempt and satisfy you – you'll never be disappointed!

Italian Bread Pudding

This deliciously rich pudding is cooked with cream and apples and is delicately flavoured with orange.

Serves 4

INGREDIENTS

15 g/^{1}/$_2$ oz/1 tbsp butter
2 small eating apples, peeled, cored
   and sliced into rings
75 g/2^3/$_4$ oz granulated sugar

2 tbsp white wine
100 g/3^1/$_2$ oz bread, sliced with
   crusts removed (slightly stale
   French baguette is ideal)

300 ml/^{1}/$_2$ pint/1^1/$_4$ cups single
   (light) cream
2 eggs, beaten
pared rind of 1 orange, cut into
   matchsticks

1 Lightly grease a 1.2 litre/ 2 pint deep ovenproof dish with the butter.

2 Arrange the apple rings in the base of the dish. Sprinkle half of the sugar over the apples.

3 Pour the wine over the apple slices. Add the slices of bread, pushing them down with your hands to flatten them slightly.

4 Mix the cream with the eggs, the remaining sugar and the orange rind and pour the mixture over the bread. Leave to soak for 30 minutes.

5 Bake the pudding in a preheated oven, at 180°C/ 350°F/Gas Mark 4, for 25 minutes until golden and set. Serve warm.

COOK'S TIP

Single (light) cream is the type of cream most commonly used for cooking. However, this type of cream should not be boiled as it will curdle. Also, always add hot liquids to the cream rather than the cream to the liquids, in order to avoid curdling. Single (light) cream has an 18 per cent fat content.

VARIATION

For a variation, try adding dried fruit, such as apricots, cherries or dates, to the pudding, if you prefer.

Tuscan Pudding

*These baked mini-ricotta puddings are delicious served warm
or chilled and will keep in the refrigerator for 3–4 days.*

Serves 4

INGREDIENTS

15 g/$^1/_2$ oz/1 tbsp butter
75 g/2$^3/_4$ oz mixed dried fruit
250 g/9 oz ricotta cheese

3 egg yolks
50 g/1$^3/_4$ oz caster (superfine) sugar
1 tsp cinnamon

finely grated rind of 1 orange, plus
   extra to decorate
crème fraîche (soured cream),
   to serve

1 Lightly grease 4 mini pudding basins or ramekin dishes with the butter.

2 Put the dried fruit in a bowl and cover with warm water. Leave to soak for 10 minutes.

3 Beat the ricotta cheese with the egg yolks in a bowl. Stir in the caster (superfine) sugar, cinnamon and orange rind and mix to combine.

4 Drain the dried fruit in a sieve set over a bowl. Mix the drained fruit with the ricotta cheese mixture.

5 Spoon the mixture into the basins or ramekin dishes.

6 Bake in a preheated oven, at 180°C/350°F/Gas Mark 4, for 15 minutes. The tops should be firm to the touch but not brown.

7 Decorate the puddings with grated orange rind. Serve warm or chilled with a dollop of crème fraîche (soured cream).

VARIATION

Use the dried fruit of your choice for this delicious recipe.

COOK'S TIP

Crème fraîche (soured cream) has a slightly sour, nutty taste and is very thick. It is suitable for cooking, but has the same fat content as double (heavy) cream. It can be made by stirring cultured buttermilk into double (heavy) cream and refrigerating overnight.

Cream Custards

Individual pan-cooked cream custards are flavoured with nutmeg and topped with caramelized orange sticks.

Serves 4

INGREDIENTS

450 ml/16 fl oz/2 cups single (light) cream
100 g/3¾ oz caster (superfine) sugar

1 orange
2 tsp grated nutmeg
3 large eggs, beaten

1 tbsp honey
1 tsp cinnamon

1 Place the cream and sugar in a large non-stick saucepan and heat gently, stirring, until the sugar caramelizes.

2 Finely grate half of the orange rind and add it to the pan along with the nutmeg.

3 Add the eggs to the mixture in the pan and cook over a low heat for 10–15 minutes, stirring constantly. The custard will eventually thicken.

4 Strain the custard through a fine sieve, into 4 shallow serving dishes. Leave to chill in the refrigerator for 2 hours.

5 Meanwhile, pare the remaining orange rind and cut it into matchsticks.

6 Place the honey and cinnamon in a pan with 2 tablespoons of water and heat gently. Add the orange rind to the pan and cook for 2–3 minutes, stirring, until the mixture has caramelized.

7 Pour the mixture into a bowl and separate out the orange sticks. Leave to cool until set.

8 Once the custards have set, decorate them with the caramelized orange rind and serve.

COOK'S TIP

The cream custards will keep for 1–2 days in the refrigerator. Decorate with the caramelized orange rind just before serving.

Sicilian Orange & Almond Cake

This is a light and tangy citrus cake better eaten as a dessert than as a cake.
It is especially good served after a large meal.

Serves 8

INGREDIENTS

4 eggs, separated
125 g/4^1/$_2$ oz caster (superfine)
  sugar, plus 2 tsp for the cream
finely grated rind and juice of
  2 oranges

finely grated rind and juice of
  1 lemon
125 g/4^1/$_2$ oz ground almonds
25 g/1 oz self-raising flour

200 ml/7 fl oz/^{3}/$_4$ cup whipping
  (light) cream
1 tsp cinnamon
25 g/1 oz flaked (slivered) almonds,
  toasted
icing (confectioners') sugar, to dust

1 Grease and line the base of a 18 cm/7 inch round deep cake tin (pan).

2 Blend the egg yolks with the sugar until the mixture is thick and creamy. Whisk half of the orange rind and all of the lemon rind into the egg yolks.

3 Mix the juice from both oranges and the lemon with the ground almonds and stir into the egg yolks. The mixture will become quite runny at this point. Fold in the flour.

4 Whisk the egg whites until stiff and gently fold into the egg yolk mixture.

5 Pour the mixture into the tin (pan) and bake in a preheated oven, at 180°C/350°F/Gas Mark 4, for 35–40 minutes, until golden and springy to the touch. Leave to cool in the tin (pan) for 10 minutes and then turn out. It is likely to sink slightly at this stage.

6 Whip the cream to form soft peaks. Stir in the remaining orange rind, cinnamon and sugar.

7 Once the cake is cold, cover with the toasted almonds, dust with icing (confectioners') sugar and serve with the cream.

VARIATION

You could serve this cake with a syrup. Boil the juice and finely grated rind of 2 oranges, 75 g/2^3/$_4$ oz caster (superfine) sugar and 2 tbsp of water for 5–6 minutes until slightly thickened. Stir in 1 tbsp of orange liqueur just before serving.

Orange & Grapefruit Salad

Sliced citrus fruits with a delicious almond and honey dressing make an unusual and refreshing dessert.

Serves 4

INGREDIENTS

2 grapefruit, ruby or plain
4 oranges
pared rind and juice of 1 lime

4 tbsp runny honey
2 tbsp warm water

1 sprig of mint, roughly chopped
50 g/1³/4 oz chopped walnuts

1 Using a sharp knife, slice the top and bottom from the grapefruits, then slice away the rest of the skin and pith.

2 Cut between each segment of the grapefruit to remove the fleshy part only.

3 Using a sharp knife, slice the top and bottom from the oranges, then slice away the rest of the skin and pith.

4 Cut between each segment of the oranges to remove the fleshy part. Add to the grapefruit.

5 Place the lime rind, 2 tablespoons of lime juice, the honey and the warm water in a small bowl. Whisk with a fork to mix the dressing.

6 Pour the dressing over the segmented fruit, add the chopped mint and mix well. Leave to chill in the refrigerator for 2 hours for the flavours to mingle.

7 Place the chopped walnuts on a baking tray (cookie sheet). Lightly toast the walnuts under a preheated medium grill (broiler) for 2–3 minutes until browned.

8 Sprinkle the toasted walnuts over the fruit and serve.

VARIATION

Instead of the walnuts, you could sprinkle toasted almonds, cashew nuts, hazelnuts or pecans over the fruit, if you prefer.

Zabaglione

This well-known dish is really a light but rich egg mousse flavoured with Marsala.

Serves 4

INGREDIENTS

5 egg yolks
100 g/3¹/₂ oz caster (superfine) sugar

150 ml/ 5 fl oz/²/₃ cup Marsala or
sweet sherry

amaretti biscuits, to serve (optional)

1 Place the egg yolks in a large mixing bowl.

2 Add the caster (superfine) sugar to the egg yolks and whisk until the mixture is thick and very pale and has doubled in volume.

3 Place the bowl containing the egg yolk and sugar mixture over a saucepan of gently simmering water.

4 Add the Marsala or sherry to the egg yolk and sugar mixture and continue whisking until the foam mixture becomes warm. This process may take as long as 10 minutes.

5 Pour the mixture, which should be frothy and light, into 4 wine glasses.

6 Serve the zabaglione warm with fresh fruit or amaretti biscuits, if you wish.

VARIATION

Iced or Semifreddo Zabaglione can be made by following the method here, then continuing to whisk the foam while standing the bowl in cold water. Beat 150 ml/ ¹/₄ pint/²/₃ cup whipping (light) cream until it just holds its shape. Fold into the foam and freeze for about 2 hours, until just frozen.

VARIATION

Any other type of liqueur may be used instead of the Marsala or sweet sherry, if you prefer. Serve soft fruits, such as strawberries or raspberries, with the zabaglione – it's a delicious combination!

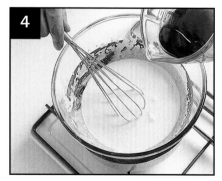

Sweet Mascarpone Mousse

A sweet cream cheese dessert that complements the
tartness of fresh summer fruits rather well.

Serves 4

INGREDIENTS

450 g/1 lb mascarpone cheese
100 g/3$^{1}/_{2}$ oz caster (superfine) sugar

4 egg yolks
400 g/14 oz frozen summer fruits,
such as raspberries and redcurrants

redcurrants, to garnish
amaretti biscuits, to serve

1 Place the mascarpone cheese in a large mixing bowl. Using a wooden spoon, beat the mascarpone cheese until smooth.

2 Stir the egg yolks and sugar into the mascarpone cheese, mixing well. Leave the mixture to chill in the refrigerator for about 1 hour.

3 Spoon a layer of the mascarpone mixture into the bottom of 4 individual serving dishes. Spoon a layer of the summer fruits on top. Repeat the layers in the same order, reserving some of the mascarpone mixture for the top.

4 Leave the mousses to chill in the refrigerator for about 20 minutes. The fruits should still be slightly frozen.

5 Serve the mascarpone mousses with amaretti biscuits.

COOK'S TIP

Mascarpone (sometimes spelled mascherpone) is a soft, creamy cheese from Italy. It is becoming increasingly more available, and you should have no difficulty finding cartons in your local supermarket, or Italian delicatessen.

VARIATION

Try adding 3 tablespoons of your favourite liqueur to the mascarpone cheese mixture in step 1, if you prefer.

Lemon Mascarpone Cheesecake

The mascarpone gives this baked cheesecake a wonderfully tangy flavour.

Serves 8

INGREDIENTS

50 g/1³/4 oz/1¹/2 tbsp unsalted butter
150 g/5¹/2 oz ginger biscuits
  (cookies), crushed

25 g/1 oz stem ginger (candied),
  chopped
500 g/1 lb 2 oz mascarpone cheese

finely grated rind and juice of 2 lemons
100 g/3¹/2 oz caster (superfine) sugar
2 large eggs, separated
fruit coulis (see Cook's Tip), to serve

1 Grease and line the base of a 25 cm/10 inch spring-form cake tin (pan) or loose-bottomed tin (pan).

2 Melt the butter in a pan and stir in the crushed biscuits (cookies) and chopped ginger. Use the mixture to line the tin (pan), pressing the mixture about 6 mm/¹/4 inch up the sides.

3 Beat together the cheese, lemon rind and juice, sugar and egg yolks until smooth.

4 Whisk the egg whites until they are stiff and fold into the cheese and lemon mixture.

5 Pour the mixture into the tin (pan) and bake in a preheated oven, at 180°C/350°F/Gas Mark 4, for 35–45 minutes until just set. Don't worry if it cracks or sinks – this is quite normal.

6 Leave the cheesecake in the tin (pan) to cool. Serve with fruit coulis (see Cook's Tip).

VARIATION

Ricotta cheese can be used instead of the mascarpone to make an equally delicious cheesecake. However, it should be sieved before use to remove any lumps.

COOK'S TIP

Fruit coulis can be made by cooking 400 g/14 oz fruit, such as blueberries, for 5 minutes with 2 tablespoons of water. Sieve the mixture, then stir in 1 tablespoon (or more to taste) of sifted icing (confectioners') sugar. Leave to cool before serving.

Tiramisu

This is a traditional chocolate dessert from Italy, although at one time it was known as Zuppa Inglese *because it was a favourite with the English society living in Florence in the 1800's.*

Serves 6

INGREDIENTS

300 g/10^1/$_2$ oz dark chocolate
400 g/14 oz mascarpone cheese
150 ml/5 fl oz/^{2}/$_3$ cup double (heavy) cream, whipped until it just holds its shape

400 ml/14 fl oz black coffee with 50 g/1^3/$_4$ oz caster (superfine) sugar, cooled
6 tbsp dark rum or brandy

36 sponge fingers (lady-fingers), about 400 g/14 oz
cocoa powder, to dust

1 Melt the chocolate in a bowl set over a saucepan of simmering water, stirring occasionally. Leave the chocolate to cool slightly, then stir it into the mascarpone and cream.

2 Mix the coffee and rum together in a bowl. Dip the sponge fingers (lady-fingers) into the mixture briefly so that they absorb the liquid but do not become soggy.

3 Place 3 sponge fingers (lady-fingers) on 3 serving plates.

4 Spoon a layer of the mascarpone and chocolate mixture over the sponge fingers (lady-fingers).

5 Place 3 more sponge fingers (lady-fingers) on top of the mascarpone layer. Spread another layer of mascarpone and chocolate mixture and place 3 more sponge fingers (lady-fingers) on top.

6 Leave the tiramisu to chill in the refrigerator for at least 1 hour. Dust with a little cocoa powder just before serving.

COOK'S TIP

Tiramisu can also be served semi-frozen, like ice-cream. Freeze the tiramisu for 2 hours and serve immediately as it defrosts very quickly.

VARIATION

Try adding 50 g/1^3/$_4$ oz toasted, chopped hazelnuts to the chocolate cream mixture in step 1, if you prefer.

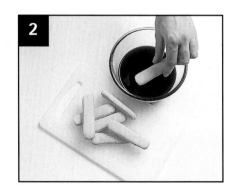

Rich Chocolate Loaf

Another rich chocolate dessert, this loaf is very simple to make and can be served as a tea-time treat as well.

Makes 16 slices

INGREDIENTS

150 g/5$^1/_2$ oz dark chocolate
75 g/2$^3/_4$ oz/6 tbsp butter, unsalted
1 x 210 g/7$^1/_4$ oz tin condensed milk

2 tsp cinnamon
75 g/2$^3/_4$ oz almonds
75 g/2$^3/_4$ oz amaretti biscuits, broken

50 g/1$^3/_4$ oz dried no-need-to-soak apricots, roughly chopped

1 Line a 675 g/1$^1/_2$ lb loaf tin (pan) with a sheet of kitchen foil.

2 Using a sharp knife, roughly chop the almonds.

3 Place the chocolate, butter, milk and cinnamon in a heavy-based saucepan. Heat gently over a low heat for 3–4 minutes, stirring with a wooden spoon, until the chocolate has melted. Beat the mixture well.

4 Stir the almonds, biscuits and apricots into the chocolate mixture in the pan, stirring with a wooden spoon, until well mixed.

5 Pour the mixture into the prepared tin (pan) and leave to chill in the refrigerator for about 1 hour or until set.

6 Cut the rich chocolate loaf into slices to serve.

COOK'S TIP

To melt chocolate, first break it into manageable pieces. The smaller the pieces, the quicker it will melt.

COOK'S TIP

When baking or cooking with fat, butter has the finest flavour. If possible, it is best to use unsalted butter as an ingredient in puddings and desserts, unless stated otherwise in the recipe. 'Low-fat' spreads are not suitable for cooking.

Pear & Ginger Cake

This deliciously buttery pear and ginger cake is ideal for tea-time
or you can serve it with cream for a delicious dessert.

Serves 4–6

INGREDIENTS

200 g/7 oz/14 tbsp unsalted butter, softened
175 g/6 oz caster (superfine) sugar
175 g/6 oz self-raising flour, sifted

3 tsp ginger
3 eggs, beaten
450 g/1 lb dessert (eating) pears, peeled, cored and thinly sliced

1 tbsp soft brown sugar

1 Lightly grease and line the base of a deep 20.5 cm/8 inch cake tin (pan).

2 Using a whisk, combine 175 g/6 oz of the butter with the sugar, flour, ginger and eggs and mix to form a smooth consistency.

3 Spoon the cake mixture into the prepared tin (pan), levelling the surface.

4 Arrange the pear slices over the cake mixture. Sprinkle with the brown sugar and dot with the remaining butter.

5 Bake in a preheated oven, at 180°C/350°F/Gas Mark 4, for 35–40 minutes or until the cake is golden and feels springy to the touch.

6 Serve the pear and ginger cake warm, with ice cream or cream, if you wish.

COOK'S TIP

To test whether the cake is cooked through, insert a fine metal skewer into the centre of the cake. If the skewer comes out clean the cake is cooked through.

COOK'S TIP

Soft, brown sugar is often known as Barbados sugar. It is a darker form of light brown soft sugar.

Peaches in White Wine

A very simple but incredibly pleasing dessert, which is especially good for a dinner party on a hot summer day.

Serves 4

INGREDIENTS

4 large ripe peaches
2 tbsp icing (confectioners') sugar, sifted

pared rind and juice of 1 orange

200 ml/7 fl oz/³/₄ cup medium or sweet white wine, chilled

1 Using a sharp knife, halve the peaches, remove the stones and discard them. Peel the peaches, if you prefer. Slice the peaches into thin wedges.

2 Place the peach wedges in a glass serving bowl and sprinkle over the sugar.

3 Using a sharp knife, pare the rind from the orange. Cut the orange rind into matchsticks, place them in a bowl of cold water and set aside.

4 Squeeze the juice from the orange and pour over the peaches together with the wine.

5 Leave the peaches to marinate and chill in the refrigerator for at least 1 hour.

6 Remove the orange rind from the cold water and pat dry with paper towels.

7 Garnish the peaches with the strips of orange rind and serve immediately.

COOK'S TIP

There is absolutely no need to use expensive wine in this recipe, so it can be quite economical to make.

COOK'S TIP

The best way to pare the rind thinly from citrus fruits is to use a potato peeler.

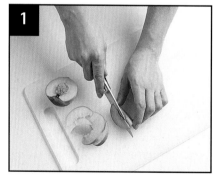

Vanilla Ice Cream

Italy is synonomous with ice cream. This home-made version of real vanilla ice cream is absolutely delicious and so easy to make.

Serves 4–6

INGREDIENTS

600 ml/1 pint/2½ cups double (heavy) cream
1 vanilla pod

pared rind of 1 lemon
4 eggs, beaten

2 egg, yolks
175 g/6 oz caster (superfine) sugar

1 Place the cream in a heavy-based saucepan and heat gently, whisking. Add the vanilla pod, lemon rind, eggs and egg yolks and heat until the mixture reaches just below boiling point.

2 Reduce the heat and cook for 8–10 minutes, whisking the mixture continuously, until thickened.

3 Stir the sugar into the cream mixture, set aside and leave to cool.

4 Strain the cream mixture through a sieve.

5 Slit open the vanilla pod, scoop out the tiny black seeds and stir them into the cream.

6 Pour the mixture into a shallow freezing container with a lid and freeze overnight until set. Serve when required.

COOK'S TIP

Ice cream is one of the traditional dishes of Italy. Everyone eats it and there are numerous gelato *stalls selling a wide variety of flavours, usually in a cone. It is also serve in scoops, and even sliced!*

COOK'S TIP

To make tutti frutti ice cream, soak 100 g/3½ oz mixed dried fruit, such as sultanas, cherries, apricots, candied peel and pineapple, in 2 tablespoons of Marsala or sweet sherry for 20 minutes. Follow the method for vanilla ice cream, omitting the vanilla pod, and stir in the Marsala or sherry-soaked fruit in step 5, just before freezing.

Granita

A delightful end to a meal or a refreshing way to cleanse the palate between courses, granitas are made from slushy ice rather than frozen solid, so they need to be served very quickly.

Serves 4

INGREDIENTS

LEMON GRANITA:
3 lemons
200 ml/7 fl oz/³/₄ cup lemon juice
100 g/3¹/₂ oz caster (superfine) sugar
500 ml/18 fl oz/2¹/₄ cups cold water

COFFEE GRANITA:
2 tbsp instant coffee
2 tbsp sugar
2 tbsp hot water
600 ml/1 pint/2¹/₂ cups cold water
2 tbsp rum or brandy

1 To make lemon granita, finely grate the lemon rind. Place the lemon rind, juice and caster (superfine) sugar in a pan. Bring the mixture to the boil and leave to simmer for 5-6 minutes or until thick and syrupy. Leave to cool.

2 Once cooled, stir in the cold water and pour into a shallow freezer container with a lid. Freeze the granita for 4–5 hours, stirring occasionally to break up the ice. Serve as a palate cleanser between dinner courses.

3 To make coffee granita, place the coffee and sugar in a bowl and pour over the hot water, stirring until dissolved.

4 Stir in the cold water and rum or brandy.

5 Pour the mixture into a shallow freezer container with a lid. Freeze the granita for at least 6 hours, stirring every 1–2 hours in order to create a grainy texture. Serve with cream after dinner, if you wish.

COOK'S TIP

If you would prefer a non-alcoholic version of the coffee granita, simply omit the rum or brandy and add extra instant coffee instead.

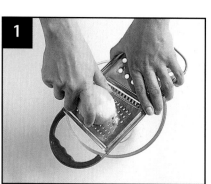

Index

Index compiled by Hilary Bird.